YORK NOTES

York Notes Rapid Revision

The Strange Case of Dr Jekyll and Mr Hyde

AQA GCSE English Literature

Written by Anne Rooney

Pearson

YORK PRESS

YORK PRESS
322 Old Brompton Road, London SW5 9JH

PEARSON EDUCATION LIMITED
80 Strand, London, WC2R 0RL

10 9 8 7 6 5 4 3 2 1

ISBN 978–1–2922–7089–0

Phototypeset by Carnegie Book Production
Printed in Slovakia

Photo credits:
GL Archive/Alamy for page 4 top / Mimadeo/Shutterstock for page 6 top /
Oshchepkov Konstantin/Shutterstock for page 8 bottom, page 26 top and
page 58 top / Ysbrand Coslin/Shutterstock for page 10 bottom and page 36
top / Podolnava Elena/Shutterstock for page 12 middle, page 34 top and page
52 middle / Kerry Shaw Brown/Stockimo/Alamy for page 14 bottom and page
30 top / OlgaLis/Shutterstock for page 16 top / peetery/© iStock for page 20
middle and page 60 top / duncan1890/© iStock for page 22 middle / Rodichey
Vitalii/Shutterstock for page 24 bottom / Robcartorres/Shutterstock for page
28 middle / vsbrandcosijn/© iStock for page 32 top, page 52 bottom and page
58 bottom / meshaphoto/© iStock for page 36 bottom / double p/© iStock for
page 38 top / Panther Media GmbH/Alamy for page 38 bottom / INTERFOTO/
Alamy for page 42 middle / chrisbrignell/© iStock for page 44 middle /
powerofforever/© iStock for page 46 middle / Brian A Jackson/Shutterstock
for page 48 top / Dmitriis Kaminskis/Shutterstock for page 50 bottom / Sergey
Novikov/Shutterstock for page 56 bottom

CONTENTS

INTRODUCTION

Who was Robert Louis Stevenson?   4
Plot summary   5

PLOT AND STRUCTURE

Chapters 1–3   6
Chapters 4–6   8
Chapters 7–8   10
Chapter 9   12
Chapter 10   14
Form and structure   16
Quick revision   18

SETTING AND CONTEXT

Victorian London and the Gothic   20
Science   22
Settings   24
Quick revision   25

CHARACTERS

Dr Jekyll in Chapters 1–7   26
Dr Jekyll in Chapters 8–10   28
Mr Hyde   30
Mr Utterson   32
Dr Lanyon   34
Poole and Mr Enfield   36
Minor characters   38
Quick revision   40

THEMES

Duality   42
Good and evil   44
Science   46
The law   48
Reputation and secrecy   50
Friendship   52
Quick revision   54

LANGUAGE

Imagery and vocabulary   56
Narrative style and voice   58
Mood and atmosphere   60
Quick revision   61

EXAM PRACTICE

Understanding the exam   62
Character questions   64
Planning your character response   66
Grade 5 annotated sample answer   68
Grade 7+ annotated sample answer   70
Theme questions   72
Planning your theme response   74
Grade 5 annotated sample answer   76
Grade 7+ annotated sample answer   78
Practice questions   80

GLOSSARY   82

ANSWERS   83

Three key things about Robert Louis Stevenson

1. He first studied **engineering**, then trained in the **law**, but became a **writer** instead of a lawyer.
2. He had **fragile health** throughout his life, and travelled in search of a healthy climate.
3. Brought up as a strict Christian, he disappointed his parents by giving up his **religion** as a young man.

What was his early life like?

- He was born in Edinburgh, in Scotland. His father was a Calvinist (a type of Protestant), and his mother was from a family of religious ministers.
- His father was an engineer and owned a company which built lighthouses. He wanted Stevenson to follow him.
- Stevenson hated studying engineering, and wanted to be a writer. His father persuaded him to study law first.

Why did Stevenson write *The Strange Case of Dr Jekyll and Mr Hyde*?

- He wrote the novel as a **shilling shocker** – a short book that would be sold cheaply – when he needed money.
- Stevenson was ill and in debt. The idea for the book came to him in a dream, and he wrote the novel in three days.
- He burned the first draft when his wife, Fanny, said he had missed the point of his own **allegory**. He rewrote it in another three days.

What was the response to *The Strange Case of Dr Jekyll and Mr Hyde*?

- The book was an instant bestseller, and Stevenson's money problems were over.
- It was so popular that **pirate copies** appeared in America, and it was translated into other languages without Stevenson's permission.
- Some religious figures even preached sermons about the book and its depiction of evil.

INTRODUCTION Plot summary

Chapters 1–3

- Mr Utterson is walking with his friend Mr Enfield, who tells him a strange tale about a violent character called Mr Hyde.
- Utterson is Dr Jekyll's lawyer, and recognises Hyde as the person Jekyll has left his possessions to.
- Utterson waits by Hyde's door and confronts Hyde, who is rude.
- Jekyll refuses to discuss Hyde with Utterson.

Chapters 4–6

- A year later, Hyde violently murders Sir Danvers Carew in the street. Utterson identifies the victim.
- Utterson leads the police to Hyde's home, but he has disappeared.
- Utterson visits Jekyll, finding him sick and distressed. Jekyll says he will have no more to do with Hyde.
- Utterson visits Dr Lanyon, who has fallen out with Hyde. Lanyon is very ill and dies soon after.

Chapter 9

- Lanyon's letter for Utterson explains how Jekyll had asked Lanyon to fetch chemicals from his laboratory and give them to Hyde.
- Hyde came to Lanyon's home, mixed the chemicals and drank the mixture.
- Hyde turned into Jekyll. The shock led to Lanyon's death.

Chapters 7–8

- Utterson and Enfield see Jekyll at his window, but a terrible look crosses Jekyll's face and he shuts the window.
- Jekyll's butler, Poole, calls on Utterson at night because he believes Hyde has murdered Jekyll.
- Utterson and Poole break down the door to Jekyll's cabinet.
- They find Hyde's body, but no trace of Jekyll. There is a document for Utterson.

Chapter 10

- Jekyll's document explains how he became convinced that human nature is divided and can be separated into two identities.
- He made a potion that turned him into Hyde, who was evil.
- The transformations went out of control. He ran out of chemicals, and could no longer turn back to Jekyll.

PLOT AND STRUCTURE Chapters 1-3

Five key things about Chapters 1-3

The first three chapters introduce the main **characters**, the main **mystery** in the story and some key **themes**:

1. We meet **Mr Utterson**, a lawyer. Stevenson tells the story from his **point of view**.
2. Other important characters are introduced: **Dr Jekyll**, **Mr Lanyon**, **Mr Hyde** and **Mr Enfield**.
3. We learn that **Hyde** is a **mysterious** and **unnatural** character with some link to **Jekyll**. Jekyll is a **scientist**, and a friend and client of **Utterson's**. Utterson aims to uncover the **link**.
4. The dark **setting** in gloomy **Victorian London** is introduced.
5. Important themes are introduced: **science**, **friendship**, **secrecy**, and **good and evil**.

What happens in Chapter 1?

- The story begins as Utterson walks with his friend Enfield through London.
- Enfield tells Utterson about a scene he saw: an unnatural-looking man trampled a small child, then went through a door the pair have just passed.
- The man returned with money to make the witnesses keep quiet. The man is called Mr Hyde.
- Utterson knows Jekyll has left his property to Hyde in his will and is curious. The will is strange, saying Hyde will come into the inheritance if Jekyll dies or disappears.

What happens in Chapters 2 and 3?

- **Chapter 2:** Determined to find out who Hyde is, Utterson visits Dr Lanyon, a friend of both Jekyll and Utterson. He learns that Lanyon and Jekyll have fallen out over Jekyll's strange ideas.
- Utterson sets out to see Hyde, and waits by the door Enfield showed him. He meets Hyde, who is rude and seems **'hardly human'**.
- Utterson imagines that Hyde is blackmailing Jekyll over something in Jekyll's past.
- **Chapter 3:** Utterson visits Jekyll and says he has met Hyde. Jekyll refuses to talk about Hyde or his will.

Five key quotations

1. Utterson's character: 'backward in sentiment; lean, long, dusty, dreary and yet somehow lovable' (Chapter 1)

2. Enfield's account of Hyde's character: 'the man trampled calmly over the child's body and left her screaming on the ground' (Chapter 1)

3. Utterson's reaction to Hyde: 'hitherto unknown disgust, loathing and fear' (Chapter 2)

4. Dr Lanyon on the theme of friendship: 'Henry Jekyll became too fanciful for me. He began to go wrong, wrong in mind.' (Chapter 2)

5. Jekyll to Utterson on the theme of secrecy: '"this is a private matter, and I beg of you to let it sleep"' (Chapter 3)

Note it!

The novel has a fragmented structure. It is pieced together from what Utterson observes or guesses, and information from other characters. For example, Enfield, a minor character, witnesses Hyde trampling a child, but Utterson does not.

Exam focus

How can I write about character?

You can use the first three chapters to write about how characters are introduced.

The first chapters introduce Utterson and show his relationships with Enfield, Lanyon and Jekyll. We learn Utterson is 'backward in sentiment; lean, long, dusty, dreary and yet somehow lovable'. The last point is surprising – it doesn't seem to fit with the others. We then see him interact with Enfield, Jekyll and Lanyon, who all respect and value him, bearing out the point made in the quotation.

> Introduces topic with a clear statement

> Quotation summarises character

> Interrogation of quotation

> Evidence of Stevenson's consistency

Now you try!

Finish this paragraph about another character. Use one of the quotations from the list.

Another character introduced in the opening chapters is Hyde. We first see him through Enfield's account of ....

Five key things about Chapters 4–6

Chapters 4–6 happen a year later than the opening chapters. The mystery becomes more complex and interesting, and aspects of **language**, **style** and **setting** are developed:

1. The murder of **Sir Danvers Carew** is told as if by the **maid**, in words that could be taken from her statement to the police. This continues the pattern of extra **narratives** that describe events **Utterson** does not see.

2. The Gothic **style** is developed in the journey to **Hyde**'s lodgings. The city is half-hidden by the **fog**, and Stevenson uses heightened **language**.

3. The **setting** of Jekyll's **laboratory** is introduced.

4. When **Mr Guest** finds **similarities** between the **handwriting of Jekyll** and **Hyde**, the link between the two characters becomes more **mysterious**.

5. The death of **Lanyon** and **Jekyll's reaction** to it increase the **mystery**.

What happens in Chapter 4?

- The maid is the only witness to Carew's murder.
- Carew was carrying a letter for Utterson, so the police contact him. Utterson goes with Inspector Newcomen to Hyde's lodgings and meets Hyde's unpleasant landlady.
- Hyde has left his lodgings hurriedly, leaving behind half of the cane used to murder Carew.

What happens in Chapters 5 and 6?

- **Chapter 5:** Utterson visits Jekyll, who is sick and distressed. Jekyll says he will have no more to do with Hyde and gives him a letter, supposedly from Hyde.

- **Chapter 5:** Utterson shows the letter to Guest, an expert in handwriting. Guest compares it with a note from Jekyll and says the writing is similar. Utterson assumes Jekyll forged the note.

- **Chapter 6:** Utterson visits Lanyon, who is very ill. Lanyon says he never wants to hear about Jekyll again.

- **Chapter 6:** Lanyon dies, leaving a package Utterson must not open yet. Jekyll will not speak to Utterson, deepening the sense of mystery.

Five key quotations

1. Style of narrative from the maid's point of view: 'never had she felt more at peace with all men or thought more kindly of the world' (Chapter 4)

2. Gothic atmosphere: 'like a district of some city in a nightmare' (Chapter 4)

3. Heightened language: 'The fog still slept on the wing above the drowned city, where the lamps glimmered like carbuncles' (Chapter 5)

4. Setting, Jekyll's laboratory: 'the tables laden with chemical apparatus, the floor strewn with crates' (Chapter 5)

5. Increasing mystery – Jekyll: '"I have brought on myself a punishment and a danger that I cannot name."' (Chapter 5)

Note it!

The letter Lanyon leaves for Utterson carries the instruction that it should not be read until the **'death or disappearance'** of Jekyll (Chapter 6). The reference to 'disappearance' also occurs in Jekyll's will. It is clear Lanyon knows something about the mystery that Utterson has not yet learned.

Exam focus

How can I write about the Gothic?

You can use Utterson's journey in Chapter 4 to write about Gothic aspects.

The account of Utterson's journey through London is	Introduces the point
evidence of the novel's reflection of Gothic literature. It is characterised by things half-seen, glimpses through the fog, and strange, unworldly scenes. London looks	Quotation illustrates a point of style
'like a district of some city in a nightmare' populated by poor, ragged children and women drinking gin in the early morning. The fog, darkness, mystery and	Further demonstrates the character of the passage
otherworldliness of the scene are typical of Gothic literature.	Ties the evidence firmly to the theme

Now you try!

Finish this further paragraph about Gothic aspects of the novel. Use one of the quotations from the list.

Another feature of the Gothic is explored in in Jekyll's account of his misery. He has ....

PLOT AND STRUCTURE Chapters 7-8

Five key things about Chapters 7-8

The action comes to a **climax**. Poole asks Utterson to go to Jekyll's house; they break down the cabinet door and find Hyde's body.

1. **Utterson** realises that **something terrible** is happening to **Jekyll** when he and **Enfield** speak to Jekyll through his window.

2. It becomes clear that the **unnaturalness** of **Hyde** is so extreme that he is **barely human**. He becomes the focus of **fear** as **Poole** believes he has **murdered Jekyll**.

3. Stevenson uses **Poole** to give information to **Utterson** and to trigger the **final action**.

4. The importance of **science** in the narrative increases as we learn of **Jekyll**'s **desperate search** for a particular **chemical**.

5. The **mystery deepens** with Hyde's **suicide** and the likely death of **Jekyll**.

What happens in Chapter 7?

- Utterson and Enfield again pass the battered door that Hyde used.
- They go into the courtyard and speak to Jekyll at his window, but Jekyll is suddenly overcome by something and his expression shows **'abject terror and despair'**. Utterson and Enfield are horrified.

What happens in Chapter 8?

- Poole visits Utterson at night, to demand that he come to Jekyll's house. Poole is worried about Jekyll, who has not been seen for days.

- Jekyll's staff are afraid that Hyde is in the house and has murdered Jekyll.

- Poole tells Utterson that Jekyll has tried to get a chemical he needs and that a figure like Hyde has been seen scurrying around.

- Poole and Utterson break down the door to Jekyll's cabinet and find the body of Hyde **'sorely contorted and still twitching'**.

- They find a note from Jekyll to Utterson, and a new will that leaves everything to Utterson. Utterson cannot understand why Hyde did not destroy the new will.

Five key quotations

1. A nameless terror strikes Jekyll: 'an expression of such abject terror and despair, as froze the very blood of the two gentlemen below' (Chapter 7)

2. Utterson indicates Poole's low social status: '"Now my good man," said the lawyer, "be explicit. What are you afraid of?"' (Chapter 8)

3. Narrative structure: '[Utterson] trudged back to his office to read the two narratives in which this mystery was now to be explained.' (Chapter 8)

4. Science: 'there were traces of chemical work, various measured heaps of some white salt being laid on glass saucers' (Chapter 8)

5. Hyde's terrifying unnaturalness: 'A dismal screech, as of mere animal terror, rang from the cabinet.' (Chapter 8)

Note it!

There is very little direct action related in the novel. Most events are told afterwards in accounts given by one of the characters, either in speech or writing. The dramatic events of the final night have additional impact because this type of action is rare.

Exam focus

How can I write about dramatic tension? AO2

These chapters can be used to explore rising tension in the novel.

> Stevenson uses the characters' terror to raise dramatic tension. Poole is afraid when he begs Utterson to come with him. Jekyll's staff are scared of whatever is now living in Jekyll's cabinet and their fear spreads to Utterson. Jekyll has a look of 'abject terror and despair, as froze the very blood of the two gentlemen'. The causes of these fears are often not stated, which creates further tension for us.

Topic sentence states the main idea	
Supporting evidence	
Quotation shows unexplained fear	
Analysis of technique	

Now you try!

Finish this further paragraph about **dramatic tension**. Use one of the quotations from the list.

Stevenson uses uncertainty about who or what is in the cabinet to raise the tension. Poole and Utterson hear a terrifying ....

Five key things about Chapter 9

Chapter 9 is the first of two chapters that **unravel the mystery**. It presents Lanyon's part of the story in the form of a **letter** Lanyon has left for Utterson:

1. **Lanyon** reveals the **terrible events** that have led to his own **death** and explains how **Jekyll** used a **potion to transform** himself into Hyde.

2. **Lanyon's letter** is another in the **series of narratives** told by **different characters** that Stevenson uses to build the novel.

3. We **see more of Hyde**, who is otherwise a shady figure for most the novel.

4. **Lanyon's character** is revealed most fully in this chapter. This is important, as he is the **counterpoint** to **Jekyll** in the novel's treatment of the **theme of science**.

5. The **theme** of **science** is explored most fully in this chapter.

What happens in this chapter?

- Lanyon's account begins with him receiving a strange letter from Jekyll.

- The letter asks Lanyon to collect a tray of chemicals from Jekyll's laboratory and keep it to give to Hyde, who will visit him at midnight.

- Lanyon believes that Jekyll has gone mad, and so he must carry out Jekyll's wishes as he can't tell what will happen if he refuses. He collects the tray of chemicals.

- Hyde arrives and Lanyon reacts to him with **'disgustful curiosity'**.

- Hyde mixes the chemicals together, and gives Lanyon the choice of watching or not, but doesn't tell him what to expect.

What happens to Lanyon?

- Lanyon, though fearful, watches as Hyde drinks the potion and, his **'mind submerged in terror'**, witnesses the transformation.

- The final paragraph sets up further mystery, as Lanyon refuses to write down what Jekyll told him. He says only that he will never recover from the shock.

Five key quotations

1. The use of different narratives – Lanyon: 'The contents increased my wonder, for this is how the letter ran'
2. Hyde to Lanyon on the theme of good and evil: '"your sight shall be blasted by a prodigy to stagger the unbelief of Satan"'
3. Lanyon on the unnaturalness of Hyde: 'There was something abnormal and misbegotten in the very essence of the creature'
4. The fascination of science – Lanyon: 'the ebullition ceased and the compound changed to a dark purple'
5. Hyde on Lanyon's view of science: '"you who have so long been bound to the most narrow and material views"'

Note it!

Lanyon describes the effect Hyde's presence has on him as he might describe a patient's symptoms. Being near Hyde causes **'incipient rigor'** and **'a marked sinking of the pulse'**. His role as a doctor is embedded in his character.

Exam focus

How can I write about science?

You can use Chapter 9 to write about the theme of science.

> Jekyll's potion is the scientific motif at the heart of the novel. It is explored most thoroughly in this chapter. Despite his horror, Lanyon is fascinated by the chemistry as Hyde mixes the potion, being careful to describe how the reaction proceeded until 'the ebullition ceased and the compound changed to a dark purple, which faded again more slowly to a watery green'. This gives the fantastical events a basis that sounds realistic.

Topic sentence sets out the point

Introduces difficult quotation with an explanation

Quotation demonstrates the point being made

Explanation of the effect of the quotation

Now you try!

Finish this further paragraph about the **theme of science**. Use one of the quotations from the list.

Jekyll and Lanyon have different ideas about science. When Hyde speaks to Lanyon, he ....

PLOT AND STRUCTURE Chapter 10

Five key things about Chapter 10

The chapter is told in the form of Jekyll's statement, which he left for Utterson. It gives Jekyll's account of what happened:

1. The **mystery** is solved, drawing together all the **threads** of the novel and answering the **questions** it has raised.

2. **Jekyll's statement** of what happened is the last of the **separate narratives**, and Jekyll is the only one who could reveal the **final secrets**.

3. It gives insight into **Jekyll**'s **character**, what drove him to his **experiment** and **how he has been affected** by it.

4. The **themes** of **duality** and **good and evil** are explored through **Jekyll**'s use of the **potion**.

5. The **Gothic** elements of the novel reach their **climax**, as the **mystery**, **supernatural** aspects, **exploration of evil**, and **extreme** events are all brought together.

What did Jekyll do?

- Jekyll explains that he wanted to pursue shameful pleasures **without** damaging his reputation, and so he looked for a way to split his personality in two.

- He made a potion that turned him into Hyde, who embodies the **'lower elements'** of his soul. Jekyll used this to enjoy his pleasures secretly.

- After Hyde murdered Carew, Jekyll decided to stop using his potion. He had changed without intending to, though, and had to use more and more of his potion to turn back.

Why did Jekyll die?

- Jekyll ran out of a chemical he needed for the potion and new supplies didn't work. He realised that an impurity in his original supply made the potion work, but new supplies were pure.

- He knew he would one day turn into Hyde and be unable to turn back. This finally happened.

- Jekyll's statement is told with great emphasis on his suffering and despair.

Five key quotations

1. Jekyll on man's duality: 'man is not truly one, but truly two'
2. Jekyll on good and evil: 'those provinces of good and ill which divide and compound man's dual nature'
3. Jekyll's character: 'the temptation of a discovery so singular and profound, at last overcame the suggestions of alarm'
4. Hyde's character: 'his every act and thought centred on self; drinking pleasure with bestial avidity from any degree of torture to another'
5. Gothic imagery: 'that insurgent horror was knit to him closer than a wife, closer than an eye; lay caged in his flesh'

Note it!

Utterson is not mentioned in this final chapter. His role is completely at an end. Although the statement was left for him to read, we do not see his response to either this statement or the letter that Lanyon left for him and that forms Chapter 9.

Exam focus

How can I write about human duality?

You can use Chapter 10 to write about the theme of duality.

> Jekyll wanted to find a way of separating what he saw as two different aspects of his nature. His philosophical and scientific work led him to the conclusion that 'man is not truly one, but truly two'. His potion bears this out, as it separates good and evil parts. He goes on to think that the human spirit might eventually turn out to have many more than two identities fused together.

Introduces main point

Jekyll's view is grounded in serious thinking

Quotation summarises Jekyll's view of the issue

How Jekyll's view develops over time

Now you try!

Finish this paragraph about the **theme** of good and evil. Use one of the quotations from the list.

The theme of good and evil is further explored in Chapter 10. Through the division of Jekyll ....

PLOT AND STRUCTURE Form and structure

Three key things about form and structure

1. The novel borrows from several forms: the **Gothic novel**, **crime novel**, **short story** and even the **epistolary** novel.

2. The story is pieced together from **narratives** by different people and from different **points of view**. This is a common feature of **Gothic** novels.

3. The last two chapters **reinterpret** earlier events. They reveal the **mystery** at the novel's heart and we see everything in a new light.

How does Stevenson use different points of view in telling the story?

- He uses a third-person narrator, who tells most of the story from Utterson's viewpoint. This means we can't see what other characters know or think.
- Enfield, Poole, Lanyon and Jekyll narrate parts of the story Utterson does not see.
- The whole story is set up by Enfield, who tells Utterson how Hyde trampled a child.

How does Stevenson develop mystery in the novel?

- Characters refuse to reveal information: Lanyon will not explain his disagreement with Jekyll, and Jekyll will not explain the strange terms of his will.
- Stevenson uses story-telling techniques from the Gothic tradition, such as leaving gaps in the account.
- Characters cannot explain why Hyde seems unnatural; there is something apparently unknowable at the heart of the novel.

How is the novel structured?

- It is a mixture of long and short chapters; Chapters 8–10 are much longer than Chapters 1–7.
- Each chapter relates one or more incidents, except the final one, which revisits the whole story.
- The first three chapters are set a year before the rest. There is another gap between Chapters 5 and 6, but it is dismissed quickly: **'Time ran on'**.

Five key quotations

1. Precise times: 'On the 12th, and again on the 14th, the door was shut against the lawyer.' (Chapter 6)

2. Controlling events across time – Lanyon's letter: 'for the hands of J.G. Utterson ALONE and in case of his predecease *to be destroyed unread*' (Chapter 6)

3. Dramatic moments – Utterson to Poole: '"We have come too late," he said sternly, "whether to save or punish."' (Chapter 8)

4. Delays and hesitation: 'I hesitated long before I put this theory to the test of practice.' (Jekyll, Chapter 10)

5. Lost intervals of time: 'the maid fainted. It was two o'clock when she came to herself' (Chapter 4)

Note it!

As Stevenson uses different narrators in different parts of the novel, he can keep back vital information about the action, and even be misleading. This allows him to manage readers' expectations and build suspense.

Exam focus

How can I write about Stevenson's use of documents in the novel?

You can discuss the documents left for Utterson by other characters.

Documents serve several purposes within the novel, one of which is controlling the flow of information.	Introduces point about form
Stevenson uses this to build mystery and suspense.	Further explanation
Jekyll's will sets out what must happen after his death and Lanyon leaves a document for 'J.G. Utterson ALONE and in case of his predecease to be destroyed unread'.	Quotation gives relevant example
These restrictions mean the mystery can't be solved until the characters are dead – if at all.	Explains consequences

Now you try!

Finish this paragraph about **structure**. Use one of the quotations from the list.

Stevenson borrows elements from the Gothic novel. Events are often half-seen, and there are gaps ....

1. Look at this ideas map for Chapter 4. Is there anything else you could add?

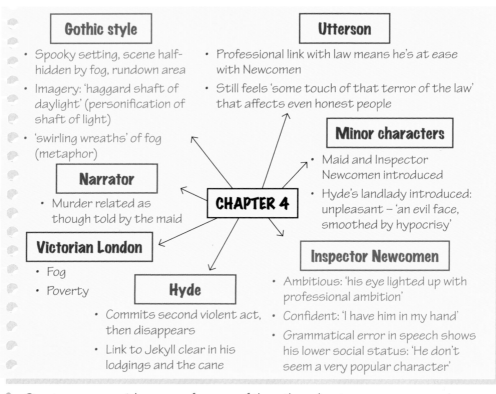

Gothic style

- Spooky setting, scene half-hidden by fog, rundown area
- Imagery: 'haggard shaft of daylight' (personification of shaft of light)
- 'swirling wreaths' of fog (metaphor)

Utterson

- Professional link with law means he's at ease with Newcomen
- Still feels 'some touch of that terror of the law' that affects even honest people

Minor characters

- Maid and Inspector Newcomen introduced
- Hyde's landlady introduced: unpleasant – 'an evil face, smoothed by hypocrisy'

Narrator

- Murder related as though told by the maid

CHAPTER 4

Victorian London

- Fog
- Poverty

Hyde

- Commits second violent act, then disappears
- Link to Jekyll clear in his lodgings and the cane

Inspector Newcomen

- Ambitious: 'his eye lighted up with professional ambition'
- Confident: 'I have him in my hand'
- Grammatical error in speech shows his lower social status: 'He don't seem a very popular character'

2. Create your own ideas map for one of the other chapters.

Quick quiz

Answer these quick questions about plot and structure.

1. What triggers Enfield's story about Hyde as he walks with Utterson?
2. How much did Hyde have to pay in compensation for trampling the girl?
3. Why is Utterson so curious about Hyde?
4. How does Utterson suspect Jekyll and Hyde are linked (Chapter 2)?
5. Who does Hyde murder?
6. How does Utterson know where Hyde lives?
7. What was the weapon Hyde used in the murder?

8. Why does Utterson show the note from Hyde to Guest?

9. Why, as we learn later, does Jekyll shrink from the window when talking to Utterson and Enfield?

10. What do Poole and Utterson use to break down the door to Jekyll's cabinet?

11. What noises has Poole heard coming from Jekyll's rooms?

12. How has Hyde killed himself?

13. In his letter to Lanyon, what does Jekyll ask him to collect from the laboratory?

14. What did Lanyon assume on the basis of Jekyll's letter?

15. What choice does Hyde give Lanyon before he takes the potion?

16. What was the first warning sign for Jekyll that his experiment was getting out of hand?

17. When did Jekyll decide to stop taking his potion?

18. Why did the potion stop working?

19. What did Jekyll decide about why his potion had worked originally?

20. How many female characters feature in the novel?

Power paragraphs

Write **a paragraph** in response to **each of these questions**. For each, try to **use one quotation** you have learned from this section.

1. How does Stevenson make use of different narrators?

2. How much of the story is explained by Dr Lanyon's letter in Chapter 9?

Exam practice

Reread the section in Chapter 2, after Utterson has spoken to Poole and wonders how Jekyll might be linked to Hyde: 'And the lawyer set out homeward … strange clauses of the will.'

Why is this moment significant in the text as a whole? Write **two paragraphs** explaining your ideas. You could comment on:

- how it relates to Utterson's character
- how Stevenson uses it to manage the mystery of the story.

Five key things about Victorian London and the Gothic

1. Victorian London was often affected by **thick fog**, called smog – a mix of fog and smoke from fires and factories.
2. **Social inequality** was severe, with some people being very **rich** and others extremely **poor**.
3. The dark, narrow streets were often the **scene of crimes**.
4. Gothic **literature** often features dark, **mysterious** and **spooky settings**.
5. Gothic literature deals with **strange happenings** and **extreme experiences**.

What was Victorian London like?

- Smog made the air difficult to breathe and often made it gloomy or dark in the daytime. It could even affect the insides of houses.
- Many buildings were in a poor state and the streets were often crowded and dirty. Coupled with the smog, this made the city dark and unhealthy.
- Some areas of the city were occupied by the very poor, and these were generally slums – with very crowded houses in a bad condition, like those which Mr Utterson passes when going to Mr Hyde's lodgings.
- The dark streets made it easy for criminals to attack people and escape, which made people afraid to go out at night.

What was London society like?

- It was important for the rich to act respectably in public, but some behaved badly in private. Dr Jekyll wants to hide behaviour he is ashamed of.
- The social classes were sharply divided. Middle-class and upper-class people had servants to look after their houses; they treated the servants as their inferiors.
- Professionals such as doctors and lawyers were well regarded and respected in society and rarely suspected of doing anything wrong.

What characterises the Gothic?

- Gothic literature often deals with topics such as the supernatural, madness, extreme passion and violence. Edgar Allan Poe's stories are an example.
- It is characterised by mystery and suspense and complex plot twists.
- Exotic settings are common, such as castles or dungeons. A scientific laboratory that had once been used for human dissection is suitably Gothic, echoing Mary Shelley's *Frankenstein*.

Three key quotations

1. The theme of reputation: 'fond of the respect of the wise and the good among my fellow-men' (Chapter 4)
2. Lanyon describing Hyde's Gothic unnaturalness: 'there was something abnormal and misbegotten in the very essence of the creature' (Chapter 9)
3. Grotesque events: 'the body of a man lay sorely contorted and still twitching' (Chapter 8)

Note it!

Inspector Newcomen is part of the London police force that was established in 1829. It struggled to combat the level of street crime. The poor were so desperate that they often had no choice but to rob people to avoid starvation.

Exam focus

How do I link context to the novel?

You can write about Stevenson's use of the Gothic.

Stevenson uses the traditions of the Gothic novel in portraying Jekyll and Hyde. Jekyll is shown experiencing extremes of terror and despair. Hyde is subhuman, with 'something abnormal and misbegotten' about him. They combine the extremes of experience and a terrifying prospect of what lies within human nature.

Clear topic statement

Successfully embedded quotation

Explanation of point

Now you try!

Finish this paragraph about the novel's **context**. Use one of the quotations from the list.

Stevenson uses the importance of reputation to explain Jekyll's motives and the ....

SETTING AND CONTEXT Science

Five key things about nineteenth-century science

1. Many people **distrusted** developments in **science** and saw them as a **threat** to their idea of what it meant to be **human**.

2. **Doctors** saw people in their **own homes** rather than in clean surgeries – **Dr Lanyon's patients** come to his **house**.

3. **Amateur science** including chemistry was a popular pastime among people (generally men) who could afford it.

4. Some **pseudo-sciences** were treated as equal to real sciences, including working out personality from handwriting (**graphology**) and how someone looks (**physiognomy**).

5. Some people saw a **conflict** between **religion** and science, a tension Stevenson explores in the novel.

What were the important developments in nineteenth-century science?

- Charles Darwin's book *On the Origin of Species*, published in 1859, argued that humans evolved from other animals. This contradicted the religious belief that God created humans.

- Advances in pharmacology (the study of drugs) showed that chemicals affect the mind and body.

- Scientists recorded their observations and experiments more systematically than in earlier times.

- Scientists began to study the workings of the mind; the first laboratory for experimental psychology opened in Germany in 1879.

What did people think about science?

- There was a strong feeling that science should avoid certain questions which threatened mainstream beliefs.

- There was little regulation of science or its products and so it was sometimes seen as dangerous.

- Some people thought science promised great things for the future, with the possibility of new discoveries improving their lives.

How does medical science relate to Stevenson's life?

- Stevenson was often unwell, and so was exposed to medical science.
- Stevenson went to university in Edinburgh, which had a famous medical school. The doctor in Chapter 1 has an Edinburgh accent.
- Stevenson was addicted to cocaine, which he took as a painkiller. Jekyll's use of the potion is presented like an addiction.

Three key quotations

1. Jekyll's scientific discovery: 'Certain agents I found to have the power to shake and to pluck back that fleshly vestment' (Chapter 10)

2. The lure of science for Jekyll: 'the temptation of a discovery so singular and profound, at last overcame the suggestions of alarm.' (Chapter 10)

3. Science as morally neutral – Jekyll: 'The drug had no discriminating action; it was neither diabolical nor divine' (Chapter 10)

Note it!

There were few effective treatments for serious illnesses, and operations were very risky. Utterson's assumption that Lanyon is ill and knows he will die is reasonable; it would be common for someone with a serious illness to know this.

Exam focus

How do I relate science to the novel?

You can write about how Stevenson explores the idea of science.

Stevenson uses science to explore the human condition. Science is supposed to be based in what can be observed and reproduced. Lanyon's description of the potion reflects this. Stevenson presents Jekyll's discovery as solid, impartial evidence: the potion itself 'was neither diabolical nor divine'. Stevenson uses the impartiality of science to suggest that Jekyll's discovery is definitely correct – science doesn't lie.	Topic statement
	Supporting evidence
	Supporting quotation successfully embedded
	Explains point

Now you try!

Finish this paragraph about the novel's **context**. Use one of the quotations from the list.

Stevenson shows the dangerous appeal of knowledge in Jekyll's experiment ....

SETTING AND CONTEXT Settings

Five key things about settings in the novel

1. All the **settings** are in London, sometimes **outdoors**, e.g. the brief trip to **Hyde's lodgings**, and at other times **within the houses** of **Jekyll**, **Lanyon** and **Utterson**.

2. The **settings** are **superficially domestic** and entirely normal, but **hide** strange, **dark deeds**.

3. Setting is linked to the themes of **reputation and secrecy** and to the internal state of the **characters**.

4. **Jekyll's house** is divided into **two distinct parts**, reflecting the **division** of his **personality**.

5. The **weather** frequently reflects events or characters' **state of mind**, with **bad weather** accompanying **misfortune and danger**.

How does Stevenson use setting to tell us about Hyde?

- Hyde is seen in the dark streets of London at night, a setting where danger and crime are common, which suits his evil, criminal behaviour.

- Hyde's lodgings are in a disreputable part of London. Utterson and Newcomen travel through grim, poverty-stricken scenes like **'some city in a nightmare'**.

What does setting reveal about the theme of reputation and secrecy?

- The outside door to Jekyll's laboratory is in a featureless, **'sinister'** and neglected building. This hides its connection with Dr Jekyll, reflecting the tension between Jekyll's respectability and his secret behaviour.

- Hyde overturns his respectably furnished lodgings, leaving the apartment Jekyll had prepared in chaos. This reflects Hyde's destructiveness and Jekyll's ordered, respectable life.

How does Stevenson use inside and outside settings?

- Outdoors is associated with danger and disorder. Hyde commits his crimes outdoors, and Jekyll first changes without the potion when he is in a park.
- Indoor settings are mostly ordered, but can become disordered under Hyde's influence. He overturns his lodgings, and Utterson and Poole break down Jekyll's door to reach him on the last night.

How does Stevenson portray Jekyll's house?

- Jekyll's house is the regular, comfortable house of a respectable citizen, with the usual domestic staff to run it.
- His laboratory is in a gloomy building hidden round the back. It was once used for dissection demonstrations, giving it grim associations.
- Above the laboratory is Jekyll's comfortable cabinet – so the building has two aspects.

Quick quiz

1. What was smog?
2. Which social problems plagued Victorian London?
3. What type of setting characterises Gothic literature?
4. Which two pseudo-sciences popular in Victorian times feature in the novel?
5. Where did doctors treat their patients in Victorian London?
6. Who did the cleaning and cooking for professional men like Lanyon and Jekyll?
7. Who proposed the theory of evolution?
8. What in Stevenson's life is reflected in Jekyll's use of his potion?
9. Give an example of another Gothic writer.
10. How did the rich behave differently in public and in private?

Power paragraphs

Choose one key **setting** or **context** related to the novel. Write **two paragraphs** explaining how Stevenson makes use of this setting or context in relation to either a) theme or b) character.

CHARACTERS Dr Jekyll in Chapters 1-7

Five key things about Dr Jekyll in the first half of the novel

1. **Jekyll** is the protagonist. He is a **medical doctor** who trained with his friend, **Dr Lanyon**.

2. There is some **mystery** surrounding Jekyll from the start, as his strange **will** leaves his property to **Mr Hyde** in the event of his **death or disappearance**.

3. His **scientific interests** are **unorthodox**, and **Lanyon** dismisses them.

4. **Jekyll** becomes very **unwell** and shuts himself away, **refusing to see anyone**.

5. He has **fallen out with Lanyon**, but neither will explain why, which deepens the **mystery** about him.

How is Jekyll introduced?

- Jekyll is introduced with an air of mystery through other characters: Mr Utterson suspects his strange will indicates madness, and Lanyon says that he is '**"wrong in mind"'**.

- He is a medical doctor and old friend of Lanyon and Utterson, though Lanyon considers his scientific work '**unscientific balderdash'**.

- We hear Utterson's guess that he is being blackmailed before we learn anything reliable about Jekyll.

- We first see him being defensive and secretive, refusing to discuss his will with Utterson.

How does Jekyll change?

- After Sir Danvers Carew's murder, Utterson finds Jekyll '**looking deadly sick'**.

- He becomes sociable again, does good deeds, and for two months seems at peace.

- Jekyll suddenly becomes sad and secretive again. He tells Utterson he chooses to be alone most of the time.

- When Utterson and Enfield see Jekyll at his window, he withdraws with '**an expression of such abject terror and despair'**.

- Poole reports that Jekyll spends his days locked in his cabinet, sending out for chemicals which he always rejects.

Five key quotations

1. Utterson on signs of Jekyll's mental stress: '"Poor Harry Jekyll," he thought, "my mind misgives me he is in deep waters!"' (Chapter 2)

2. Jekyll's appearance early on: 'a large, well-made, smooth-faced man of fifty, with something of a slyish cast perhaps, but every mark of capacity and kindness' (Chapter 3)

3. Lanyon on the changes in Jekyll: '"Henry Jekyll became too fanciful for me. He began to go wrong, wrong in mind"' (Chapter 2)

4. Jekyll's account of his interests: 'his own tastes being chemical rather than anatomical' (Chapter 5)

5. Jekyll's appearance near his death: 'close up to the warmth, sat Dr Jekyll, looking deathly sick. He did not rise to meet his visitor' (Chapter 5)

Note it!

Stevenson reveals Jekyll's sophisticated tastes in the way he decorates Hyde's lodgings and his own cabinet. Hyde's lodgings are **'furnished with luxury and good taste'**. There is a cupboard of wine, silver plates, fine table linen and a **'good picture'** on the wall.

Exam focus

How can I write about how others see Jekyll? AO1

You can comment on Utterson's thoughts and concerns about Jekyll.

> Utterson is worried about Jekyll's association with Hyde and his view of Jekyll is shown through this concern. He at first thinks the strange will is a sign of madness, but after he meets Hyde he assumes that Jekyll is being blackmailed: '"Poor Harry Jekyll," he thought, "my mind misgives me he is in deep waters!"' Through Utterson's mistaken idea, Stevenson forms our early view of Jekyll as a victim of some injustice.

Topic sentence summarises Utterson's point of view

Shows development of Utterson's view

Appropriate quotation supports the point

Explains effect of a technique

Now you try!

Finish this paragraph about Lanyon's view of Jekyll. Use one of the quotations from the list.

Lanyon surprises Utterson with his view of Jekyll ....

Five key things about Dr Jekyll in the second half of the novel

1. **Henry Jekyll** describes himself and what he has done in his final **statement**.
2. He wanted to be held in high **regard** and was **ashamed** of even minor **failings**.
3. He found a way of **separating** the parts of himself by taking a chemical **potion** that freed his worse part, embodied in **Hyde**.
4. His discovery has led to terrible **suffering** as the **evil part** unleashed in **Hyde** takes over his life.
5. He loses control of the **transformation** into **Hyde**, so that it starts to happen without the **potion**.

Why did Jekyll make and use his potion?

- He is keen to appear respectable in public and wants to hide behaviour he thought was unsuitable for a **'noted professor'**.
- He formed the idea that every person combines different aspects and that these might be separated.
- He discovered chemicals that could affect the mind and body. He experimented until he made a potion that would separate the parts of his nature.
- The potion gave him the chance to do whatever he liked. He found this thrilling and addictive.

How does Jekyll see himself?

- He was originally proud, and ashamed of faults that he felt fell short of his own high standards.
- He sees himself as a victim as well as someone who has done something wrong.
- He still thinks he has made a great, if terrible, scientific discovery.
- He recognises that the evil embodied in Hyde is part of himself.

Five key quotations

1. Jekyll's concern with his reputation: 'rather the exacting nature of my aspirations than any particular degradation in my faults' (Chapter 10)

2. Jekyll considers splitting himself: 'I had learned to dwell with pleasure, as a beloved daydream, on the thought of the separation of these elements.' (Chapter 10)

3. Jekyll's self-satisfaction: 'I smiled, comparing myself with other men, comparing my active good-will with the lazy cruelty of their neglect.' (Chapter 10)

4. Jekyll's addiction: 'It was on this side that my new power tempted me until I fell in slavery.' (Chapter 10)

5. Jekyll's self-pity: '"If I am the chief of sinners, I am the chief of sufferers also."' (Chapter 6)

Note it!

Jekyll gives up the potion after Carew's murder, but he misses what he could do as Hyde. He feels the urge to indulge his **'lower side'** but **'in my own person'**, not taking the potion. It is then that he turns into Hyde in Regent's Park.

Exam focus

How can I write about how Jekyll sees himself? AO1

You can draw on Jekyll's statement to discuss his view of himself.

> Jekyll writes his statement to explain what he has done, so it reveals a lot about how he sees himself. He tries to take away from the wrong he has done by stressing the harm he has suffered: 'If I am the chief of sinners, I am the chief of sufferers also.' He struggles to accept his responsibility for Hyde's deeds, and is unwilling to give up his good opinion of himself.

Clear statement of where evidence will come from

Explains implications of the quotation

Appropriate quotation

Further analysis of his view

Now you try!

Finish this paragraph about how Stevenson depicts Jekyll. Use one of the quotations from the list.

Stevenson offers insight into Jekyll's self-satisfaction through the words he gives him. When Jekyll says ....

Five key things about Mr Hyde

1. **Edward Hyde** is **Jekyll**'s **alter ego** (literally, his 'other self'). To start with, he exists only when Jekyll takes his **potion**, but we do not learn this until the end of the novel.

2. **Hyde** is smaller than **Jekyll**, but grows larger as Jekyll turns into him more often.

3. Everyone who meets **Hyde** finds him **repulsive**, but no one can say what is wrong with how he looks.

4. **Hyde** commits acts of **violence** and destroys things.

5. **Hyde** is associated with the **Devil**, and **Jekyll** calls him an embodiment of **pure evil**.

What do we learn about Hyde in the novel?

- He begins as a mysterious character, linked with Jekyll in some way that is not clear.

- He is immediately shown as cruel. He tramples a small child and pays off witnesses to avoid trouble.

- He is rude to Utterson when they meet, and to Lanyon later in the novel.

- Hyde vanishes and, despite searching, the police can find no reliable information about him.

- He is frequently at Jekyll's house and laboratory, where he makes Poole and the other staff feel uncomfortable.

How does Hyde change?

- At the start of the novel, Hyde is already unpleasant. He becomes aggressive when confronted after trampling the girl.

- Next he becomes more violent, murdering Carew apparently without reason.

- He becomes a stronger influence, and Jekyll starts to change into him without taking the potion.

- By the end of the novel we learn that Hyde hates Jekyll and is afraid of him, because Jekyll could destroy him by killing himself. (Jekyll's interpretation of the situation.)

Five key quotations

1. Utterson's first reaction to Hyde: '"God bless me, the man seems hardly human!"' (Chapter 2)

2. Lanyon's account of Hyde: 'there was something abnormal and misbegotten in the very essence of the creature' (Chapter 9)

3. Jekyll first turns into Hyde: 'I knew myself, at the first breath of this new life, to be more wicked, tenfold more wicked' (Chapter 10)

4. After Carew's murder: 'tales came out of the man's cruelty, at once so callous and violent, of his vile life, of his strange associates' (Chapter 6)

5. Jekyll's own account of Hyde: 'a being inherently malign and villainous; his every act and thought centered on self' (Chapter 10)

Note it!

Note that physically Hyde looks very different from Jekyll. He is short and slight, so Jekyll's clothes hang off him, looking **'ludicrous'**. His hands are small, dark, knotted and hairy, while Jekyll's are large, white and smooth.

Exam focus

How can I write about how other characters view Hyde? AO1

You can comment on how Stevenson presents other characters' reactions to Hyde.

Everyone who sees Hyde is immediately repelled by him. People can't quite identify what is wrong with how he looks, but 'There was something abnormal and misbegotten in the very essence of the creature' as Lanyon says. Enfield notices in Chapter 1 that even the doctor looks as though he wants to kill Hyde. Lanyon's words make Hyde sound less than human. He is a 'creature' and 'misbegotten', not just ugly.	Clear statement of characters' response
	Relevant quotation successfully embedded
	Further evidence cited
	Careful analysis of language

Now you try!

Finish this paragraph about how Jekyll feels about Hyde. Use one of the quotations from the list.

Jekyll is the only character who truly knows Hyde. He explains Hyde's character from the inside. When he first changes into Hyde ....

Five key things about Mr Utterson

1. **Mr Gabriel Utterson** is a **lawyer**. Both **Jekyll** and **Carew** are his **clients**.

2. Much of the novel is **narrated** from **Utterson**'s **point of view**, though not in his words.

3. **Utterson** is a stable character who **does not change** over the course of the novel.

4. He takes little part in the **action**, but he takes **Inspector Newcomen** to **Hyde**'s lodgings and breaks down the door to **Jekyll**'s cabinet with **Poole**.

5. The novel plays out around **Utterson**'s **efforts** to uncover the **mystery** of **Jekyll**'s will and the **link** between Jekyll and **Hyde**.

What do we learn about Utterson?

- He is kindly, calm and popular with his friends, although he says little.
- Utterson is a loyal friend; his friends are **'those he had known the longest'**.
- He jumps quickly to conclusions and then acts as though they were definitely correct.
- He lives a frugal life. He enjoys the theatre but doesn't go due to the cost, and he drinks gin to avoid drinking expensive wine.
- He shows little emotion, and he does not tend to pass judgement on the deeds of others.

What is Utterson's role in the novel?

- Enfield tells Utterson the story of Hyde trampling a child, introducing Hyde.
- As Jekyll's lawyer, Utterson knows about Jekyll's strange will, naming Hyde. The will and Enfield's story prompt Utterson to look for Hyde.
- Utterson knows Jekyll and Lanyon, so is well placed to draw together the threads of the story. Each leaves him a document explaining part of the mystery.
- Utterson's stable but dull personality does not intrude into the action. As people trust him, they are willing to share some information with him.

Five key quotations

1. Utterson is introduced: 'cold, scanty and embarrassed in discourse; backward in sentiment' (Chapter 1)
2. Utterson's pattern of forming friendships: 'his affections, like ivy, were the growth of time, they implied no aptness in the object' (Chapter 1)
3. Utterson is stable and conventional: 'a lover of the sane and customary sides of life' (Chapter 2)
4. Utterson's imagination follows his conclusions: '"It turns me cold to think of this creature stealing like a thief to Harry's bedside"' (Chapter 2)
5. Utterson needs human contact: 'never in his life had he been so conscious of so sharp a wish to see and touch his fellow-creatures' (Chapter 8)

Note it!

Note that Utterson's tendency to jump to conclusions is not in keeping with his job. As a lawyer, he should be patient and weigh up evidence, but he tends to seize on the first interpretation that occurs to him.

Exam focus

How can I write about the way Utterson is associated with mystery? AO1

You can comment on how Stevenson uses Utterson to uncover and also create mystery.

Stevenson uses Utterson's curiosity about who Hyde is to present and unravel the mystery in the novel. He	Clear statement of argument
also uses Utterson's incorrect guesses to mislead us and keep things hidden. When Utterson reflects that	Expands on what Stevenson is doing
'It turns me cold to think of this creature stealing like a thief to Harry's bedside', the vividness of the image	Appropriate embedded quotation
encourages us to accept his suggestion without thinking about whether it's correct.	Explains effect of literary technique

Now you try!

Finish this paragraph about how Stevenson presents Utterson as a friend in the novel. Use one of the quotations from the list.

Utterson is a friend of Dr Jekyll and Dr Lanyon. Stevenson shows him interacting ....

Five key things about Dr Lanyon

1. **Dr Hastie Lanyon** is a **medical doctor** who trained with **Dr Jekyll**.

2. **Lanyon** has **fallen out** with **Jekyll** over their different views of **science**.

3. **Lanyon** has a **practical**, **down-to-earth** approach to **science**. He is concerned with conditions and effects that can be **observed** and **measured**.

4. **Lanyon** is the only person to see the process of **transformation** as **Hyde** changes to **Jekyll**.

5. **Lanyon** leaves a **document** for **Utterson** which reveals that **transformation** is the **link** between **Jekyll** and **Hyde**.

What do we learn about Dr Lanyon?

- Lanyon went to school with Utterson; Lanyon and Utterson are **'the oldest friends'** Jekyll has.

- In Chapter 6, Lanyon considers himself **'a doomed man'** with just weeks to live.

- He thinks Jekyll's research is **'unscientific balderdash'**, and Jekyll considers him unimaginative, with **'narrow and material'** views.

- Early in the novel he is lively and the way he shows his feelings is **'somewhat theatrical to the eye'**.

How does Lanyon change?

- Lanyon and Jekyll were once **'inseparable friends'** but have since fallen out. By the end of the novel, he will not even talk about Jekyll.

- Initially, he is strong and healthy, but later becomes pale, older-looking and frail, with a **'trembling hand'**.

- Lanyon has enjoyed life, but after witnessing the transformation he is disillusioned and, with what he now knows, would be **'more glad to get away'** from life.

- He can't survive the challenge to his worldview, or believe what he has seen; he will **'die incredulous'**.

Five key quotations

1. Lanyon is introduced: 'a hearty, healthy, dapper, red-faced gentleman, with a shock of hair prematurely white, and a boisterous and decided manner' (Chapter 2)

2. Lanyon of his disagreement with Jekyll: '"I beg that you will spare me any allusion to one whom I regard as dead."' (Chapter 6)

3. Lanyon has changed: 'The rosy man had grown pale; his flesh had fallen away; he was visibly balder and older' (Chapter 6)

4. Resignation to his fate: '"life has been pleasant; I liked it; yes, sir, I used to like it"' (Chapter 6)

5. Impact of seeing Hyde's transformation: 'My life is shaken to its roots; sleep has left me; the deadliest terror sits by me at all hours' (Chapter 9)

Note it!

Note that although Lanyon is afraid of what will happen when Jekyll's messenger arrives, he acts bravely. He sends his servants to bed and loads a revolver, which he keeps beside him in case the encounter becomes dangerous.

Exam focus

How can I write about Dr Lanyon's decline and death?

You can comment on how Stevenson presents change in Lanyon.

> Early in the novel, Lanyon is healthy, confident and cheerful. Later, we see him physically and emotionally changed. He becomes older, weaker and afraid, and is certain that he will die soon. In his own words, 'My life is shaken to its roots; sleep has left me; the deadliest terror sits by me at all hours.' He is unable to process what he has seen, and can't reconcile it with his view of the world.

Concise account of Lanyon's initial state

Statement of how Lanyon changes

Use of appropriate quotation

Explanation of reason for change

Now you try!

Finish this paragraph about Lanyon's relationship with Jekyll. Use one of the quotations from the list.

Lanyon and Jekyll are old friends, but Lanyon has fallen out with him because ....

Three key things about Poole

1. **Poole** is **Jekyll**'s faithful **butler**, and works in Jekyll's house.
2. He is the only character who sees **Hyde** regularly.
3. He is a **working man**, and of **lower social class** than all the main characters, but is of **higher status** than the other servants in **Jekyll's household**.

What is Poole's function in the novel?

- Stevenson uses Poole to pass on information about what happens in Jekyll's house when none of the other characters is there to see it.
- Poole fetches Utterson on the last night and they break down the door together. He triggers the only dramatic act that happens in real time in the novel, rather than being told after the event.
- Poole is the only lower-class character given any development; he is the only representative of this large part of Victorian society.

Three key things about Mr Enfield

1. **Mr Richard Enfield** is a **cousin** and **friend** of **Utterson's**; he goes on regular Sunday **walks** with Utterson.
2. He sees and **reports** the incident when **Hyde trampled** over a **small child**.
3. He is sociable, a **man of action**, and people think him an unlikely friend for Utterson.

What is Enfield's function in the novel?

- Enfield tells the story about Hyde, introducing the revulsion experienced by everyone who sees him.
- On Enfield's second walk with Utterson, they see the terrible expression on Jekyll's face just before he transforms into Hyde. This is the first glimpse of Jekyll's mysterious suffering.
- Stevenson shows Utterson's character through his walks with Enfield, including how he slowly develops friendships with different types of people.

Five key quotations

1. Poole at Utterson's house: 'he sat with the glass of wine untasted on his knee, and his eyes directed to a corner of the floor' (Chapter 8)

2. Poole upset by Jekyll/Hyde's distress: '"I came away with that upon my heart, that I could have wept too."' (Chapter 8)

3. Poole questioning Jekyll's behaviour: 'why did he cry out like a rat, and run from me? I have served him long enough.' (Chapter 8)

4. Enfield is related to Utterson: a 'distant kinsman, the well-known man about town' (Chapter 1)

5. Enfield chases after Hyde: '"I gave a view halloa, took to my heels, collared my gentleman, and brought him back"' (Chapter 1)

Note it!

Poole's language reveals his status as lower than that of Utterson and Jekyll. He uses phrases like 'I don't know rightly how to say it' and calls Utterson 'sir'. His informal language communicates emotion well, e.g. when he says that hearing Hyde weeping made him feel like weeping himself.

Exam focus

How can I write about Poole's character? AO1

You can comment on how Stevenson shows Poole's relationship with Jekyll.

Poole is a loyal employee; he is genuinely concerned about Jekyll and knows him well. Poole uses rhetorical questions to show Utterson that the thing in the laboratory is unlike Jekyll. He asks '"Why did he cry out like a rat, and run from me? I have served him long enough."' This shows that Poole would feel hurt if Jekyll behaved like this, as he knows him so well.

Topic statement

Introduces point to be illustrated by quotation

Appropriate quotation

Explains effect of quotation

Now you try!

Finish this paragraph about Mr Enfield. Use one of the quotations from the list.

Mr Enfield's role in the novel relies on his relationship with Utterson. He tells the story of how he runs after Hyde, presenting himself ....

My progress   Needs more work ☐   Getting there ☐   Sorted! ☐   37

CHARACTERS Minor characters

Five key things about minor characters

1. **Sir Danvers Carew**, like **Jekyll**, is a legal client of **Utterson**.
2. **Inspector Newcomen** relishes **Carew**'s murder, as it offers a **professional opportunity** for him.
3. Hyde's **landlady** is **pleased** to hear that **Hyde** is in trouble.
4. Stevenson tells **Carew's murder** from the **maid's point of view**, in **language** that she might have used in a statement.
5. **Mr Guest** is **Utterson**'s head **clerk**. He **can interpret** personality from **handwriting** and **finds a** similarity between the handwriting of **Jekyll** and **Hyde**.

What is the role of minor characters?

- Stevenson uses the maid to describe the murder of Carew, which none of the main characters sees.
- Inspector Newcomen goes with Utterson to Hyde's lodgings, allowing the reader to see inside Hyde's home and discover a further link with Jekyll.
- Mr Guest leads Utterson to think Jekyll forged Hyde's letter – another false clue that keeps the mystery going.

How does Stevenson represent different social classes?

- The maid and Hyde's landlady are of lower social class.

- Inspector Newcomen and Mr Guest have respectable jobs, but are of lower class than the main characters.
- Sir Danvers Carew is of higher social class than the main characters.

How does Stevenson use minor characters to develop themes?

- The idealised description of Carew through the maid's eyes reinforces the conventional portrayal of respect for the upper class from the lower class.
- Jekyll chose Hyde's landlady as someone **'silent and unscrupulous'**, a demonstration of the care he has taken to cover his tracks.
- Guest's expertise in the pseudo-science of graphology is an aspect of the theme of science.

Five key quotations

1. Sir Danvers Carew: 'an innocent and old-world kindness of disposition, yet with something high too, as of a well-founded self-content' (Chapter 4)

2. The maid's mood before the murder: 'never had she felt more at peace with all men or thought more kindly of the world' (Chapter 4)

3. Utterson's relationship with Mr Guest: 'There was no man from whom he kept fewer secrets than Mr Guest' (Chapter 5)

4. Hyde's landlady: 'She had an evil face, smoothed by hypocrisy; but her manners were excellent.' (Chapter 4)

5. Newcomen's reaction to Carew's murder: 'his eye lighted up with professional ambition. "This will make a deal of noise"' (Chapter 4)

Note it!

Stevenson typically uses minor characters only once. They each have one characteristic which helps them fulfil their role, and there is no sense of a complex personality. For instance, Guest is used only to interpret handwriting and lead Utterson to a false assumption.

Exam focus

How can I write about minor characters? AO1

You can comment on how Stevenson matches the nature of Hyde's landlady to her role.

Jekyll has chosen Hyde's landlady as someone who will turn a blind eye to his behaviour in return for money. She 'had an evil face, smoothed by hypocrisy, but her manners were excellent'. This is just what Jekyll needs. The importance of her nature becomes clear later in the novel, when we learn Jekyll was planning carefully to cover his tracks as Hyde.

Information about her character

Appropriate quotation

Explains how her character suits her role

Further analysis of how appropriateness is revealed

Now you try!

Finish this paragraph about Mr Guest. Use one of the quotations from the list.

Mr Guest is Utterson's head clerk. While he is Utterson's social inferior ....

1. Look at this ideas map relating to Mr Utterson. Is there anything else you could add?

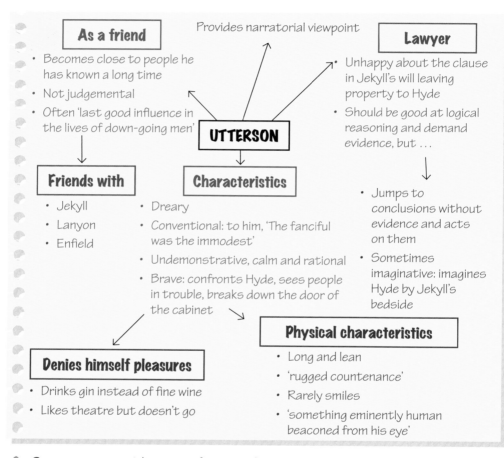

Provides narratorial viewpoint

As a friend
- Becomes close to people he has known a long time
- Not judgemental
- Often 'last good influence in the lives of down-going men'

Lawyer
- Unhappy about the clause in Jekyll's will leaving property to Hyde
- Should be good at logical reasoning and demand evidence, but ...

UTTERSON

Friends with
- Jekyll
- Lanyon
- Enfield

Characteristics
- Dreary
- Conventional: to him, 'The fanciful was the immodest'
- Undemonstrative, calm and rational
- Brave: confronts Hyde, sees people in trouble, breaks down the door of the cabinet

- Jumps to conclusions without evidence and acts on them
- Sometimes imaginative: imagines Hyde by Jekyll's bedside

Denies himself pleasures
- Drinks gin instead of fine wine
- Likes theatre but doesn't go

Physical characteristics
- Long and lean
- 'rugged countenance'
- Rarely smiles
- 'something eminently human beaconed from his eye'

2. Create your own ideas map for one of the other characters.

Quick quiz

Answer these quick questions about character.
1. Who does Hyde murder?
2. How does Jekyll want to appear to other people?
3. What does Lanyon think about Jekyll's state of mind?

4. Which character is described as 'lean, long, dusty, dreary'?

5. What is Lanyon's profession?

6. Who does Utterson go walking with on Sundays?

7. What are Hyde's clothes like?

8. Why does Utterson have Jekyll's will?

9. Why is Inspector Newcomen especially keen to find the murderer?

10. What characteristics of the landlady drew Jekyll to choose her lodgings for Hyde?

11. Who is the most upper-class character in the novel?

12. What is Jekyll's view of Lanyon's approach to science?

13. What is the name of Jekyll's butler?

14. What does Utterson think is the connection between Jekyll and Hyde?

15. Why does Utterson show Guest Hyde's letter?

16. Who is described as 'an aged and beautiful gentleman'?

17. Why does Utterson go to ask Lanyon if he has come across Hyde?

18. Why does Lanyon's physical appearance change?

19. What is Utterson's attitude towards simple pleasures?

20. Why does Hyde fear Jekyll?

Power paragraphs

Write **a paragraph in response to each of these questions**. For each, try to **use one quotation** you have learned from this section.

1. How do other characters respond to Hyde?

2. What role does Stevenson give Mr Enfield in the novel?

Exam practice

Reread the section in Chapter Eight starting '"Sir", said the butler ... murder done"' in which Poole tells Utterson he thinks Jekyll has been murdered.

Why is this moment significant in the text as a whole? Write **two paragraphs** explaining your ideas. You could comment on:

● what it tells us about Poole

● what it tells us about Poole's view of Jekyll/Hyde.

THEMES Duality

Five key things about the theme of duality

1. **Duality** is explored through **Dr Jekyll splitting his personality** using his **potion**.
2. Stevenson examines the idea that **human nature** includes contrasting **rational** and **instinctive** parts.
3. **Mr Hyde** acts selfishly, following his **instincts** for pleasure, but **Jekyll** is **rational**, keeping his instincts under control.
4. **Jekyll** recognises that his **rational behaviour** and the **appetites** and **desires** of **Hyde** are **equal** parts of himself.
5. **Jekyll** finally suggests that there may be **more than two** parts to **human nature**.

What is the duality of human nature, and how is it shown?

- The duality of human nature can be described as two contrasting urges – to follow a desire and to control it.
- For thousands of years, this duality has been seen as a conflict between the pleasure-seeking body and the rational mind, or between body and soul.
- Jekyll describes two aspects of human nature constantly battling within each of us.
- Jekyll remains the rational part of himself.
- Hyde is concerned only with his own pleasure; he embodies the selfish, instinctive drives.

Why and how does Jekyll challenge the duality of his nature?

- Jekyll feels he has to hide some of his behaviour to appear respectable.
- Jekyll is troubled by having to repress his appetite for **'undignified'** pleasures. This leads him to try to separate the parts of his nature.
- He makes a potion that releases Hyde, an alter ego (literally, 'another self') that follows his lowest desires.
- After giving his pleasure-seeking side free rein, Jekyll loses his ability to control it.
- The lesson from Jekyll's experience is that the contrasting aspects of human nature are always in tension, and trying to break the tension is fatal.

Five key quotations

1. Jekyll's account of duality: 'man is not truly one, but truly two' (Chapter 10)
2. Jekyll on Hyde: 'a being inherently malign and villainous; his every act and thought centred on self' (Chapter 10)
3. Jekyll struggles with duality: 'It was the curse of mankind that these incongruous faggots were thus bound together' (Chapter 10)
4. His response to Hyde: 'I was conscious of no repugnance, rather of a leap of welcome. This, too, was myself.' (Chapter 10)
5. Jekyll's conclusion about human nature: 'man will be ultimately known for a mere polity of multifarious, incongruous and independent denizens' (Chapter 10)

Note it!

Note that other people are repulsed by Hyde because he seems unnatural. He is unnatural because he represents the savage aspect of human nature. Normally, the part Hyde symbolises is kept in check by human reason.

Exam focus

How does Stevenson explore duality? AO1

You can write about how Stevenson uses the potion to explore duality.

Stevenson explores duality through Jekyll's use of the potion to divide the two aspects of his nature. The division is into a rational part that exercises control and an irrational, passionate part that follows instincts. Hyde represents the part that is entirely selfish and driven by appetites, while Jekyll retains the rational part. Stevenson suggests that every person has warring aspects within them, and balancing them is normal and necessary.

- Topic statement
- Clear definition
- Shows how theme is treated in the novel
- Statement of Stevenson's central idea in the novel

Now you try!

Finish this paragraph about duality. Use one of the quotations from the list.

Stevenson demonstrates the duality of human nature by splitting Jekyll into two characters. Jekyll struggles with this but eventually recognises that it is ....

Five key things about the theme of good and evil

1. **Hyde** is associated with **evil** throughout the novel, and Jekyll refers to him as **'pure evil'**.

2. Evil is set against good symbolically in **Hyde**'s attacks on two characters. The **small girl** and **Sir Danvers Carew** are presented as entirely **innocent** and **good**.

3. The novel links **evil** with basic human **instincts for pleasure**.

4. Good and evil are presented within a **Christian framework**, with **Hyde** linked with **Satan**.

5. The struggle between parts of **Jekyll's character** can be seen in terms of a **struggle between good and evil**.

Why do good and evil become central to the novel?

- Stevenson presents Hyde as inhumanly evil from the start, and he is the focus of the novel's mystery.

- Hyde is associated with evil and the other characters oppose him; this makes the action look like a battle against evil.

- Stevenson uses religious language that puts Jekyll in the role of a Christian and Hyde as Satan. This recalls the struggle between good and evil at the heart of Christianity.

- Stevenson suggests that each person is a mix of good and evil, and this puts the struggle within everyone.

How are good and evil presented outside the Jekyll/Hyde pair?

- Mr Utterson thinks about the bad things he has done or nearly done in the past as he considers whether Hyde is blackmailing Jekyll.

- Hyde's landlady is unpleasant, perhaps evil; Carew and the trampled girl are portrayed as good or innocent.

- Dr Lanyon, a good man, is fatally shocked by the level of evil revealed to him by Jekyll.

- The **'undignified'** pleasures Jekyll wants to hide from public view are never revealed, so we are uncertain how bad they really are.

Five key quotations

1. Jekyll on Hyde's evil: 'alone in the ranks of mankind, was pure evil' (Chapter 10)
2. Jekyll on the mix of good and evil: 'all human beings, as we meet them, are commingled out of good and evil' (Chapter 10)
3. Utterson on Hyde's evil: '"if ever I read Satan's signature upon a face, it is on that of your new friend"' (Chapter 2)
4. Sir Danvers Carew: 'seemed to breathe such an innocent and old-world kindness of disposition' (Chapter 4)
5. Lanyon: '"O God!" I screamed, and "O God!" again and again' (Chapter 9)

Note it!

Note that as Utterson travels with Inspector Newcomen to Hyde's lodgings, the area is presented as nightmarish. It is referred to as **'blackguardly'** or villainous. The suggestion is that the people living here, such as the women drinking gin in the early morning, are lacking in morals.

Exam focus

How does Stevenson explore the theme of good and evil in the novel? AO1

You can write about the split of good and evil within Jekyll.

> Stevenson explores the theme of good and evil by dividing Jekyll into two, the relatively good Jekyll and the utterly evil Hyde. Once Jekyll can do what he likes as Hyde, he lives respectably as himself and does good deeds, becoming a better person. Hyde, on the other hand, 'alone in the ranks of mankind, was pure evil'. Given free rein, Hyde grows more powerful. Stevenson shows that unrestrained evil will grow.

Describes basic technique

Demonstrates point working in the novel

Suitable quotation competently embedded

Explains effect Stevenson achieves

Now you try!

Finish this paragraph about the theme of good and evil. Use one of the quotations from the list.

Stevenson shows that all people are a mix of good and evil. Jekyll discovers as a result of his fatal experiment that ....

Five key things about the theme of science

1. **Lanyon** and **Jekyll** are both **scientists**. Jekyll carries out experiments in his laboratory, and Lanyon is a medical doctor who sees patients at his house.

2. **Jekyll** is scornful of **Lanyon**'s **practical**, **down-to-earth** science, while Lanyon dismisses Jekyll's brand of science as **fanciful** and **'unscientific'**.

3. It is through science that **Jekyll transforms** himself into **Hyde**.

4. **Jekyll**'s dependence on his **potion**, first for pleasurable excursions as **Hyde** and later to be normal (to remain himself), follows the pattern of **drug addiction**, a problem Stevenson had himself.

5. The novel raises questions about the **dangers** and **opportunities** science brings to humankind.

How does Stevenson explore the theme of science?

- Stevenson offers contrasting ideas about science through Jekyll and Lanyon so they can be compared and played off against each other.

- Lanyon's focus on observable physical states makes Jekyll's transformation a terrible shock to him.

- Jekyll explores new territory in his experiment.

- Lanyon thinks Jekyll's work **'unscientific'**. This raises the question of how science can be defined.

- Jekyll's science is presented as dangerous. Through it, Stevenson uses Jekyll's dangerous experiment to address the public fear of scientists 'playing God'.

How does Stevenson present science and scientific ideas?

- Jekyll's laboratory roots his science in practical experiments, using chemicals, glassware and other equipment.

- The last owner of Jekyll's house was a surgeon who used the laboratory for dissection demonstrations.

- Lanyon narrates the transformation of Hyde into Jekyll, reporting both the chemical reaction and the change in Hyde in careful scientific detail.

- Stevenson makes reports of fantastic events more convincing by stressing the precise details of his scientific material.

Five key quotations

1. Lanyon on Hyde mixing the potion: 'measured out a few minims of the red tincture and added one of the powders' (Chapter 9)

2. Lanyon chooses to watch the transformation: '"I have gone too far in the way of inexplicable services to pause before I see the end."' (Chapter 9)

3. Lanyon's view of Jekyll's science: '"Such unscientific balderdash"' (Chapter 9)

4. Hyde criticises Lanyon: '"you who have denied the virtue of transcendental medicine"' (Chapter 9)

5. Jekyll's cabinet: 'At one table there were traces of chemical work, various measured heaps of some white salt being laid on glass saucers' (Chapter 8)

Note it!

The novel returns repeatedly to the idea that someone's moral character is shown in their appearance, the subject of physiognomy. Hyde looks abnormal, and this is a sign in the novel that he is evil.

Exam focus

Exploring the limits of science?

You can write about how Stevenson uses precise language to explore the limits of science.

Stevenson uses scientific language to present Jekyll's potion, as Hyde 'measured out a few minims of the red tincture and added one of the powders'. The potion's action is also described in precise detail. Yet mystery lies behind this precision – we don't know what is in the potion or how it is working on Jekyll. Scientific knowledge covers only the surface of things and does not get to their root.

Topic statement

Apt quotation to illustrate point

Reference to further evidence

Identifies a broader point

Now you try!

Finish this paragraph about Lanyon and science. Use one of the quotations from the list.

Lanyon is a scientist of a traditional type, focused on testable evidence. He watches Hyde take the potion because as a scientist he is curious and feels ....

THEMES The law

Five key things about the theme of the law

1. **Utterson** is a **lawyer**; the action is shown from the point of view of someone interested and experienced in the **law**.

2. **Jekyll**'s **will**, which is central to the plot, is a **legal document**. **Utterson** looks after it, and its terms give him a reason to look for **Hyde** and for Hyde to give him his address.

3. **Utterson** represents the **theoretical, desk-bound aspects** of the law.

4. **Inspector Newcomen** represents the law in its **practical, active, crime-fighting** aspect.

5. The final chapters, which unravel the **mystery**, are presented as **documents Utterson** is **legally bound** to look at only after **Jekyll**'s death.

What role does the law play in the novel?

- The terms of Jekyll's will drive Utterson's curiosity and interest in Hyde, moving the story along.

- The law directs Utterson's thoughts. When pondering the connection between Jekyll and Hyde, he jumps to conclusions that involve crimes.

- Utterson is also Sir Danvers Carew's lawyer, and Carew was carrying a letter addressed to him. This leads Inspector Newcomen to ask Utterson to identify the body.

- Jekyll stops using his potion because he is afraid that Hyde will be caught and charged with Carew's murder.

How is the law portrayed in the novel?

- Utterson is presented as stolid and dull, a **'dry lawyer'**.

- Stevenson shows the law as ineffectual and ignored. Hyde is not caught, and the people who stop Hyde after he tramples a child don't call the police.

- Inspector Newcomen sees Carew's murder as a chance to further his career.

- Poole and Utterson take matters into their own hands on the final night and only send for the police later.

Five key quotations

1. Utterson on law: 'he was conscious of some touch of that terror of the law and the law's officers, which may at times assail the most honest' (Chapter 4)

2. Reports of Hyde: 'the few who could describe him differed widely, as common observers will' (Chapter 4)

3. Utterson on forgery: '"What!" he thought. "Henry Jekyll forge for a murderer!"' (Chapter 5)

4. Newcomen on the murder: 'his eye lighted up with professional ambition. "This will make a deal of noise"' (Chapter 4)

5. Utterson tempted: 'great curiosity came on the trustee, to disregard the prohibition and dive at once to the bottom of these mysteries' (Chapter 6)

Note it!

Note that although Utterson is an honest lawyer, he thinks that Hyde **'must have secrets of his own; black secrets'**. This implies he could perhaps prevent the blackmailing of Jekyll by using these secrets – not behaviour we would expect of a lawyer.

Exam focus

How does Stevenson write about the law?

You can explore how Stevenson uses Utterson to write about the law.

> Stevenson explores the theme of the law through the character of Utterson. Utterson thinks in terms of crimes. He first fears blackmail, then later jumps to another conclusion: '"What!" he thought. "Henry Jekyll forge for a murderer!"' We trust in Utterson's ideas, but they are wrong, and Stevenson uses our trust in legal expertise and ideas to mislead us.

Statement of Utterson's relation to the theme

Explains how Stevenson uses character to support a theme

Appropriate quotation supporting a point

Relates strategy to narrative technique

Now you try!

Finish this paragraph about how Stevenson uses the law to structure the novel. Use one of the quotations from the list.

Stevenson uses a legal document, Jekyll's will, tempting Utterson to introduce the mystery about Hyde. Documents become a central motif ....

THEMES Reputation and secrecy

Five key things about the theme of reputation and secrecy

1. **Jekyll** is concerned to keep his **reputation** as a **respectable doctor**. He makes his potion so he can enjoy himself **secretly**, protecting his **reputation**.

2. There are many **secrets** in the novel; characters often refuse to discuss or **reveal** information.

3. **Blackmail**, suggested by **Utterson** as a reason for **Hyde**'s hold over **Jekyll**, relies on **secrets** and a concern with **reputation**.

4. Stevenson keeps the nature of **Jekyll**'s **'undignified'** pleasures hidden, so our own **standards of morality** don't affect our **judgement** of Jekyll.

5. **Hyde** embodies the notion of **secrecy** and **hidden evils**; his name is a play on the word 'hide'.

What does reputation mean, and how does Stevenson explore it in the novel

- Reputation means how someone is regarded by others and what is publicly known about them.
- Jekyll's reputation as a respectable man is very important to him.
- Jekyll says he is **'in no sense a hypocrite'** yet he hides his bad behaviour.
- Jekyll's concern with reputation continues when he is Hyde. He pays money to the bystanders in Chapter 1 to avoid a **'scene'**.

How is secrecy used in the novel?

- Hyde is secretive by name and by nature. He goes out at night, and scurries around in dark corners in Jekyll's house.

- Neither Jekyll nor Lanyon will explain to Utterson why they have fallen out.

- It is **ironic** that Jekyll creates Hyde to free himself from secrecy but ends up with another secret.

- Even at the end, Jekyll does not reveal what is in his potion or how it works.

- Stevenson suggests that some things must stay hidden, as knowledge of them is unbearable. Some can't be revealed because there is no language to talk about them.

Five key quotations

1. Jekyll wants to be respected: 'fond of the respect of the wise and good among my fellow-men' (Chapter 10)

2. Jekyll's pride: 'my imperious desire to carry my head high, and wear a more than commonly grave countenance before the public' (Chapter 10)

3. Jekyll on Hyde: 'he resented the dislike with which he was himself regarded' (Chapter 10)

4. Jekyll's secret predicament: 'I have brought on myself a punishment and a danger that I cannot name.' (Chapter 6)

5. Hyde's concern about trouble: '"No gentleman but wishes to avoid a scene."' (Chapter 1)

Note it!

Note that Jekyll chooses Hyde's landlady on the basis of her being someone he can trust to be **'silent and unscrupulous'**. She will keep Hyde's behaviour secret, no matter what it is like, because she wants his rent money.

Exam focus

How does Stevenson explore reputation? (AO1)

You can write about how Stevenson uses Jekyll to explore the idea of reputation.

Stevenson explores the idea of reputation through the character and actions of Jekyll. He is 'fond of the respect of the wise and good among my fellow-men' to the point that he hides pleasures he thinks threaten his respectability. Instead of giving up shameful pleasures, he finds in his potion a way to hide and continue them. Stevenson shows his behaviour as dangerous and hypocritical: Jekyll is more concerned about how he seems than how he is.

Topic sentence introduces paragraph
Quotation illustrates point
Statement of a point
Demonstration of how the point is made in the novel

Now you try!

Finish this paragraph about secrecy. Use one of the quotations from the list.

The novel is built around secrecy, mystery and things that cannot be said ....

Five key things about the theme of friendship

1. At the core of the novel are **three old friends**: **Utterson**, **Lanyon** and **Jekyll**.
2. **Lanyon** and **Jekyll** have **fallen out**, but neither will fully explain the **reason** to **Utterson**.
3. His **loyal friendship** with **Jekyll** spurs **Utterson** to find out who **Hyde** is and what **hold** he has over Jekyll.
4. **Utterson's** other friend, **Mr Enfield**, introduces him to the story of **Hyde**.
5. Despite their recent difficulties, **Jekyll relies** on **Lanyon's friendship** to bring him the tray of chemicals he needs as **Hyde**. Lanyon's act of friendship results in his death.

How does Stevenson explore the theme of friendship?

- Stevenson explores friendship through the relationships between his main characters, especially when they face difficult circumstances.
- Utterson accepts Jekyll's refusal to explain his link with Hyde. When he pushes Jekyll to tell him more it is because he fears for Jekyll's safety.
- Lanyon and Jekyll originally fell out over their different approaches to science. Despite this, Lanyon is willing to help Jekyll even when he thinks he has lost his mind.
- The nature of Utterson's friendships is described: he befriends people he knows for a long time, and sticks with them, even if they suffer misfortune.

How does Utterson's role as a friend drive the plot?

- Utterson's friend Enfield first tells him about Hyde.
- Because he is friends with Jekyll, Utterson is worried about Jekyll's link with Hyde and decides to investigate.
- Utterson remains loyal to Jekyll even when Jekyll will not answer his questions or allow his visits.
- His affection for Jekyll leads him to help Poole break down the door to the cabinet, rather than send for the police.

Five key quotations

1. How Utterson forms friendships: 'His friends were those of his own blood or those whom he had known the longest' (Chapter 1)

2. Utterson and Enfield: 'It was a nut to crack for many, what these two could see in each other' (Chapter 1)

3. Jekyll's friendship with Utterson: 'you could see by his looks that he cherished for Mr Utterson a sincere and warm affection' (Chapter 3)

4. Utterson's loyalty: 'the last reputable acquaintance and the last good influence in the lives of down-going men' (Chapter 1)

5. Jekyll's plea to Lanyon: 'my life, my honour, my reason, are all at your mercy' (Chapter 9)

Note it!

Note that the police investigation into Hyde finds that he is friendless. He has had **'few familiars'** and his family can't be traced. It is another feature that makes him seem abnormal, especially in a novel in which friendship is the only type of relationship shown.

Exam focus

How does Stevenson explore friendship? (AO1)

You can write about how Stevenson uses Utterson to develop the theme of friendship.

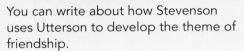

Utterson is friends with Lanyon and Jekyll, so is the focus of Stevenson's study of friendship. He is a loyal friend, yet is undiscerning in making friends. His friendship with Enfield presented 'a nut to crack for many, what these two could see in each other'. Friendship often seems contradictory: Jekyll tells Utterson he will not see him, and Utterson's final act of friendship is to disobey Jekyll and break down his door.

Topic sentence	
Further detail	
Supporting quotation	
Further point developing an idea	

Now you try!

Finish this paragraph about the friendship between Lanyon and Jekyll. Use one of the quotations from the list.

Stevenson portrays a friendship broken by a strong difference of opinion between Lanyon and Jekyll. Even so, Jekyll turns to Lanyon in despair ....

1. Look at this ideas map representing the theme of secrecy and reputation. Is there anything else you could add?

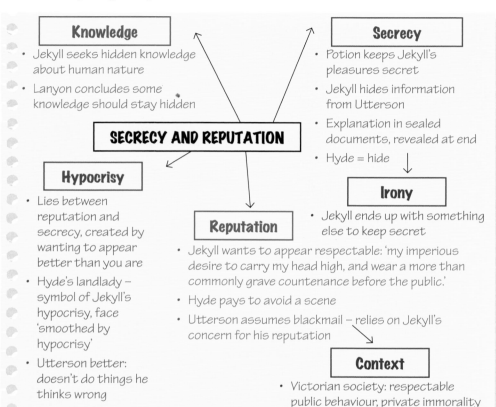

Knowledge
- Jekyll seeks hidden knowledge about human nature
- Lanyon concludes some knowledge should stay hidden

Secrecy
- Potion keeps Jekyll's pleasures secret
- Jekyll hides information from Utterson
- Explanation in sealed documents, revealed at end
- Hyde = hide

SECRECY AND REPUTATION

Hypocrisy
- Lies between reputation and secrecy, created by wanting to appear better than you are
- Hyde's landlady – symbol of Jekyll's hypocrisy, face 'smoothed by hypocrisy'
- Utterson better: doesn't do things he thinks wrong

Reputation
- Jekyll wants to appear respectable: 'my imperious desire to carry my head high, and wear a more than commonly grave countenance before the public.'
- Hyde pays to avoid a scene
- Utterson assumes blackmail – relies on Jekyll's concern for his reputation

Irony
- Jekyll ends up with something else to keep secret

Context
- Victorian society: respectable public behaviour, private immorality

2. Create your own ideas map for another theme.

Quick quiz

Answer these quick questions about themes.

1. Which characters are professionally engaged in the law?
2. Which pseudo-science is associated with Mr Guest?
3. What is Jekyll trying to protect when he makes his potion?
4. Why, at the start of the novel, have Lanyon and Jekyll fallen out?

5. Why is Utterson's friendship with Enfield considered odd?

6. Why does Hyde pay £100 to the family of the trampled child?

7. What makes Hyde's landlady a suitable choice for Jekyll?

8. What type of person does Utterson have as friends?

9. Which characters are professionally engaged in science?

10. Who is described as 'pure evil'?

11. Who is described as 'innocent' and 'beautiful'?

12. What is Jekyll's conclusion about the duality of man?

13. What type of behaviour does Jekyll want to hide?

14. Who is criticised for 'scientific heresies'?

15. Who are Jekyll's oldest friends?

16. How does Utterson know what is in Jekyll's will?

17. Why does Jekyll send Poole out repeatedly for more chemicals?

18. Why does Lanyon watch as Hyde takes the potion?

19. Why are people repulsed by Hyde?

20. What is Utterson afraid of as he travels with Inspector Newcomen?

Power paragraphs

Write **a paragraph** in response to **each of these questions**. For each, try to **use one quotation** you have learned from this section.

1. How does Jekyll's concern for his reputation lead to his downfall?

2. Does Stevenson present science as dangerous?

Exam practice

Reread the section in Chapter 10 when Jekyll decides to behave virtuously and has chosen to stop using the potion: 'I resolved in my future conduct … assaults of temptation.'

How is this moment significant in the text as a whole? Write **two paragraphs** explaining your ideas. You could comment on:

- how Stevenson depicts Jekyll's attitude to the duality of his nature here
- how the duality of Jekyll's nature is important in the novel as a whole.

LANGUAGE Imagery and vocabulary

Five key things about Stevenson's use of imagery and vocabulary

1. Stephenson uses powerful images to convey **key themes** and **issues**.
2. He uses simile and metaphor to help the **reader** understand **difficult, unfamiliar ideas**.
3. He uses heightened **language** as part of the Gothic **tradition** he draws on.
4. He uses **references** and **images** from **Christian** and **classical mythology**.
5. He uses **vocabulary** to convey aspects of **character**.

How does Stevenson use Gothic imagery and vocabulary?

- Stevenson uses heightened vocabulary to take feelings and experience to extremes. At the window, Dr Jekyll has an expression of **'abject terror and despair'**.
- He uses vivid metaphors, such as calling London a **'drowned city'**, and similes, such as lights that **'glimmered like carbuncles'**.

How does Stevenson use imagery to present unfamiliar ideas?

- He uses startling images to relate ideas that lie outside our experience. For example, Jekyll describes Mr Hyde with the metaphor **'caged in my flesh'**.
- He uses animal imagery to suggest that the appetites Hyde pursues are bestial. Jekyll's base desires **'growl for licence'**.

How does Stevenson use detailed vocabulary to create impact?

- He quickly creates an idea of a certain sort of person by combining a few carefully chosen details. Mr Utterson sees women **'passing out, key in hand, to have a morning glass'**, suggesting low morals as they rush out to get alcohol in the morning.

- His careful attention to detail gives an impression of clarity, concealing deeper mystery. Dr Lanyon says the potion began **'to effervesce audibly, and to throw off small fumes of vapour'**.

Five key quotations

1. Domestic image conveys extreme emotion – Jekyll: 'a fancy brimming with images of terror, a soul boiling with causeless hatreds' (Chapter 10)

2. Simile and metaphor communicate unfamiliar ideas – Jekyll: 'that insurgent horror was knit to him closer than a wife, closer than an eye' (Chapter 10)

3. Ornate language creates a vivid picture: 'flying wrack of the most diaphanous and lawny texture' (Chapter 8)

4. Classical reference from Enfield: 'we were keeping the women off him as best we could, for they were as wild as harpies' (Chapter 1)

5. Colloquial language conveys Poole's character: '"I don't like it, sir – I wish I may die if I like it."' (Chapter 8)

Note it!

Simple language is rarely used in the novel, but has great emotional impact when it appears. For example, Jekyll says to Utterson '"I have had a lesson – O God, Utterson, what a lesson I have had!"' The repetition stresses the intensity of his feeling.

Exam focus

How can I write about Stevenson's use of imagery? AO2

You can write about the use of heightened language to convey the unfamiliar.

Stevenson uses the heightened language and rich imagery common in Gothic literature to communicate unfamiliar ideas. Jekyll describes his horror at Hyde being 'knit to him closer than a wife, closer than an eye'.	Relates language to theme and context
	Suitable quotation illustrates point
The first image is unalarming, as a wife should be close; the second is disturbing as an eye is integral, not close.	Detailed attention to how language works
The idea of a cage of flesh, which comes straight after, is deeply troubling.	Further evidence

Now you try!

Finish this paragraph about how Stevenson uses language to convey emotion. Use one of the quotations from the list.

The novel is full of extreme emotions beyond readers' experiences. Stevenson uses language to make them more accessible, as when he uses a domestic image ....

My progress   Needs more work ☐   Getting there ☐   Sorted! ☐   **57**

LANGUAGE Narrative style and voice

Five key things about Stevenson's use of narrative style and voice

1. He uses long, **complex sentences**, often with **unfamiliar vocabulary**.
2. The narrative voice varies to show the **points of view** of different **characters** even when it does not directly use their words.
3. The documents written by **Lanyon** and **Jekyll** work as monologues, using the **distinctive voices** of each of those characters.
4. At times, Stevenson shows **language failing** to convey **deep feeling** or **unfamiliar ideas**.
5. He uses dialogue to convey the **personality** and **mood** of characters.

How does Stevenson use voice?

- Stevenson usually recounts things from Utterson's viewpoint. He uses the maid's point of view for Carew's murder, choosing language that she might have used in court: **'as she so sat, she became aware of an aged and beautiful gentleman'**.
- Lanyon's voice is measured, calm and analytical even in extreme situations.
- Jekyll's voice uses heightened language and emotion.

How does Stevenson use speech?

- Stevenson uses dialogue to build character, move the plot along and deepen the mystery. It heightens the mystery, e.g. when one character will not tell another what he wants to know.
- He uses monologue in Utterson's thoughts. These present Utterson's ideas about what is going on, which are generally wrong. Stevenson builds the mystery in this way.

How does Stevenson use sentence length?

- Stephenson gives Utterson many long sentences, some quite hard to follow. This produces a strong narrative voice, echoing the way a lawyer might speak.
- Short sentences are used mostly in speech, signalling annoyance, impatience or emotion, as when Poole snaps **'"Hold your tongue!"'** to the weeping maid.

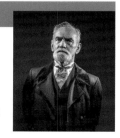

Five key quotations

1. The maid's point of view: 'stamping with his foot, brandishing the cane, and carrying on (as the maid described it) like a madman' (Chapter 4)
2. Lanyon's voice: 'He was small, as I have said; I was struck besides with the shocking expression of his face' (Chapter 9)
3. Jekyll's voice: 'The veil of self-indulgence was rent from head to foot, I saw my life as a whole' (Chapter 10)
4. Limitations of language: 'I have brought on myself a punishment and a danger that I cannot name.' (Jekyll, Chapter 6)
5. Dialogue and character: '"Ah, it's an ill-conscience that's such an enemy to rest!"' (Poole, Chapter 8)

Note it!

Although Jekyll speaks in an elevated way, Hyde speaks plainly. His language is direct and often rude. He just wants to get to the point, as when he meets Utterson and responds to his greeting with, '"That is my name. What do you want?"'

Exam focus

How can I write about Jekyll's voice? AO2

You can write about the vivid language that gives Jekyll his distinctive voice.

Stevenson gives Jekyll a distinctive voice that uses vivid imagery and high emotion well suited to his extreme experiences. Jekyll's language is dramatic and intense, reflecting his heightened emotional state. His images often include violence, such as 'the veil of self-indulgence was rent from head to foot'. His complicated sentences and the richness and intensity of his imagery are stifling.

- Clear statement of voice's characteristics
- Explains function of Stevenson's technique
- Suitable quotation to support point
- Further comment on the effect Stevenson achieves

Now you try!

Finish this paragraph about how Stevenson uses language to tell us about Poole. Use one of the quotations from the list.

Stevenson uses Poole's voice to tell us about his character and social status. Poole speaks ....

LANGUAGE Mood and atmosphere

Five key things about Stevenson's use of mood and atmosphere

1. He creates a **threatening atmosphere** through much of the novel.

2. He **contrasts** a **cosy setting** or **atmosphere** with **action** to create **impact**, as when **Carew**'s murder disturbs a peaceful evening.

3. He often matches the **weather** or **setting** to the mood of characters or events.

4. He creates an **atmosphere** of seediness and **decay** for the parts of London where **Hyde** is seen.

5. He sometimes creates a **light mood** and then **disturbs** it, as when Jekyll is sitting in the park but changes into **Hyde**.

How does Stevenson create a threatening atmosphere?

- He creates scenes where things are half-seen, where neither we nor the characters know what is happening, creating anxiety.
- He uses a gloomy setting, marked by decay, poverty, and hostile or unfriendly people.
- He uses bad or threatening weather, such as the fog that forms **'swirling wreaths'** or the **'biting weather'** on the last night that has the wind **'lashing'** the trees along the railing.

How does Stevenson occasionally create a cosy atmosphere?

- He piles up details that describe a pleasant scene, such as the wine, silver plates and pictures in Hyde's lodgings.
- He uses cheerful words in his descriptions, as when the fire **'chatters'** and the kettle is **'singing'** in Jekyll's cabinet.

How does Stevenson use dialogue to create a sense of foreboding?

- He has characters hint at something bad happening in the near future, as when Lanyon says that they shall not live to make other friends.
- Characters express hopelessness, but without giving a proper explanation for it.

How does Stevenson use language to communicate mood?

- He uses expressive verbs. Lanyon **'sprang up'** from his chair and **'welcomed'** Utterson **'with both hands'**; this conveys the energy and enthusiasm of his greeting.

- He uses rhythm and patterns to create mood. The changes in Lanyon are described in short, slow clauses that each go down in pitch and a have a dull, slowing rhythm: **'The rosy man had grown pale; his flesh had fallen away; he was visibly balder and older'.**|

Quick quiz

1. How is the evening described immediately before the murder of Carew?
2. Who uses heightened language and unusual imagery?
3. What stylistic device does Poole use to persuade Utterson that he has seen Hyde in the laboratory?
4. When Stevenson describes Utterson and Poole turning over Hyde's body, he refers to the body as 'it'; what effect does this have?
5. What does Stevenson show by having Utterson call Poole 'my good man'?
6. Who uses an abrupt and aggressive tone of voice?
7. What literary technique is Stevenson using in 'the fortress of identity'?
8. What impression of Jekyll's home is created by it being 'warmed' by a 'bright open fire'?
9. What literary technique is Stevenson using here: 'Edward Hyde would pass away like the stain of breath upon a mirror'?
10. Utterson says to Guest, '"I wouldn't speak of this note, you know."' Why does he phrase it like this?

Power paragraphs

Choose one aspect of the way Stevenson uses language. Write **two paragraphs** explaining how Stevenson makes use of this in relation to either a) theme or b) character.

Five key things about the exam

1. You will have **one** question on *Dr Jekyll and Mr Hyde* which will be based on an **extract** given to you on the exam paper.

2. It will focus on **Stevenson's presentation** of an aspect of the novel, such as a **character**, **relationship** or **theme**.

3. You will have about **45–50 minutes** to read and respond to the question.

4. The question is worth **30 marks**.

5. The question assesses **AOs 1, 2 and 3**. Remember that **AO3** relates to '**context**'.

What will a question look like?

1. Read the extract in Chapter 6 when Utterson visits Lanyon: 'There at least he was not denied admittance … to get away."'

> You must refer to the given passage

Starting with this extract, explore how Stevenson presents changes in Lanyon's character during the novel.

> You must explain the techniques Stevenson uses

> This is the area you must tackle

Write about:

- how Stevenson shows changes in Lanyon's character in this extract

> A reminder to begin with the given passage/ extract

- how Stevenson presents changes in Lanyon's character in the novel as a whole.

[30 marks]

> A reminder to **also** write about the whole of the novel

Do all questions look the same?

- Not all questions will begin this way. Some might contain statements you must argue with or against. For example, **'Stevenson's presentation of Utterson leads us to trust him.' Starting with this extract, explore how far you agree with this opinion.**

- Not all questions will be about a single character. Some might ask you about a **relationship** between two characters, e.g. between Jekyll and Utterson.

What do I need to do to get a good mark?

Use this grid to understand what your current level is and how to improve it:

	AO1 Read, understand, respond	**AO2** Analyse language, form, structure and effects	**AO3** Show understanding of contexts
High	• You make **precise references** to the **passage** and *Dr Jekyll and Mr Hyde* **as a whole**. • Your **argument** is well-structured, with quotations **fluently embedded** in sentences. • You cover **both** the extract and the whole novel.	• You **analyse** and **interpret** the methods Stevenson uses **very effectively**. • You **explore thoughtfully** the effects of these on the reader. • You show **excellent use** of subject terminology.	• You make **detailed, relevant links** between specific elements of novel and social, historical contexts.
Mid	• You make a **range of references** to the passage and the novel as a whole. • You respond in **a clear, logical way** with **relevant** quotations chosen.	• You **explain clearly** some of the methods Stevenson uses, and **some effects** on the reader. • You use **mostly relevant** subject terminology.	• You show **clear evidence** of understanding context which is **linked** to the novel in places.
Lower	• You make **some references** to the passage and novel as a whole, but in rather a **patchy** way. • You make **some useful points** but evidence is **not always clear or relevant**.	• You make **occasional attempts** to explain Stevenson's methods but these are a little **unclear**. • You show **some use** of subject terminology.	• You demonstrate **basic awareness** of context but **links** to the novel are **undeveloped** and **not always relevant**.

Read these exam-style character questions

Read this extract from Chapter 10 in which Jekyll introduces himself and the events that led to his experiment. Then answer the question that follows.

> I was born in the year 18— to a large fortune, endowed besides with excellent parts, inclined by nature to industry, fond of the respect of the wise and good among my fellow-men, and thus, as might have been supposed, with every guarantee of an honourable and distinguished future. And indeed
> 5 the worst of my faults was a certain impatient gaiety of disposition, such as has made the happiness of many, but such as I found it hard to reconcile with my imperious desire to carry my head high, and wear a more than commonly grave countenance before the public. Hence it came about that I concealed my pleasures; and that when I reached years of reflection, and began to look
> 10 round me and take stock of my progress and position in the world, I stood already committed to a profound duplicity of life. Many a man would have even blazoned such irregularities as I was guilty of; but from the high views that I had set before me, I regarded and hid them with an almost morbid sense of shame. It was thus rather the exacting nature of my aspirations than any
> 15 particular degradation in my faults, that made me what I was, and, with even a deeper trench than in the majority of men, severed in me those provinces of good and ill which divide and compound man's dual nature. In this case, I was driven to reflect deeply and inveterately on that hard law of life, which lies at the root of religion and is one of the most plentiful springs of distress. Though
> 20 so profound a double-dealer, I was in no sense a hypocrite; both sides of me were in dead earnest; I was no more myself when I laid aside restraint and plunged in shame, than when I laboured, in the eye of day, at the furtherance of knowledge or the relief of sorrow and suffering. And it chanced that the direction of my scientific studies, which led wholly towards the mystic and the
> 25 transcendental, reacted and shed a strong light on this consciousness of the perennial war among my members.

2. Starting with this extract, how does Stevenson present Jekyll as a tormented individual?

Write about:

- how Stevenson presents Jekyll in this extract
- how Stevenson presents Jekyll as tormented in the novel as a whole.

[30 marks]

Read this extract from Chapter 1 in which Stevenson introduces the character of Mr Utterson. Then answer the question that follows.

> Mr Utterson the lawyer was a man of a rugged countenance, that was never lighted by a smile; cold, scanty and embarrassed in discourse; backward in sentiment; lean, long, dusty, dreary and yet somehow lovable. At friendly meetings, and when the wine was to his taste, something eminently human
> 5 beaconed from his eye; something indeed which never found its way into his talk, but which spoke not only in these silent symbols of the after-dinner face, but more often and loudly in the acts of his life. He was austere with himself; drank gin when he was alone, to mortify a taste for vintages; and though he enjoyed the theatre, had not crossed the doors of one for twenty years. But
> 10 he had an approved tolerance for others; sometimes wondering, almost with envy, at the high pressure of spirits involved in their misdeeds; and in any extremity inclined to help rather than to reprove. 'I incline to Cain's heresy,' he used to say quaintly: 'I let my brother go to the devil in his own way.' In this character, it was frequently his fortune to be the last reputable acquaintance
> 15 and the last good influence in the lives of down-going men. And to such as these, so long as they came about his chambers, he never marked a shade of change in his demeanour.
>   No doubt the feat was easy to Mr Utterson; for he was undemonstrative at the best, and even his friendships seemed to be founded in a similar
> 20 catholicity of good-nature. It is the mark of a modest man to accept his friendly circle ready-made from the hands of opportunity; and that was the lawyer's way. His friends were those of his own blood or those whom he had known the longest; his affections, like ivy, were the growth of time, they implied no aptness in the object. Hence, no doubt the bond that united him
> 25 to Mr Richard Enfield, his distant kinsman, the well-known man about town. It was a nut to crack for many, what these two could see in each other or what subject they could find in common. It was reported by those who encountered them in their Sunday walks, that they said nothing, looked singularly dull, and would hail with obvious relief the appearance of a friend.

3. 'Stevenson presents much of the novel from Utterson's point of view, though not in his voice. Utterson's character is well suited to this role.' Starting with this extract, explore how far you agree with this opinion.

Write about:

- how Stevenson presents Utterson in this extract
- how Stevenson's presentation of Utterson in the novel as a whole suits his role. **[30 marks]**

EXAM PRACTICE Planning your character response

Five key stages to follow

1. **Read** the **question**; **highlight** key words.
2. **Read** the **extract** with the **key words** from the **question** in mind.
3. Quickly **generate ideas** for your response.
4. **Plan** for paragraphs.
5. **Write** your response; **check it** against your plan as you progress.

What do I focus on?

Highlight the **key words**:

1. Starting with this extract, how does Stevenson present Jekyll as a tormented individual?
   Write about:
   - how Stevenson presents Jekyll in this extract
   - how Stevenson presents Jekyll as tormented in the novel as a whole.

What do they tell you? Focus on both extract and whole text; explain what specific methods Stevenson uses; stick to Jekyll's torment as the main topic.

How should I read the passage?

- Check for any immediate links to the question (e.g. **'an almost morbid sense of shame'**).
- Look for any evidence/quotations you could highlight (e.g. he is aware of **'the perennial war among my members'** or parts of his personality).

How do I get my ideas?

Note your ideas in a spider diagram or list them in a table:

The extract   **The novel as a whole**

Sets himself high standards   *Suffers 'terrors so unmanning'*
he can't live up to
                        ┌─────────────────┐   *Utterson and Enfield*
                        │ **Jekyll as a** │   *appalled by his*
Feels he has two   │ **tormented man**│   *appearance at the*
warring parts   └─────────────────┘   *window*

The extract	The novel as a whole
• Is ashamed to fall short of the high standards he sets himself	• He considers himself the 'chief of sufferers'
• He feels two parts of himself are constantly at war	• After Carew's murder, he is in a very bad state
• He feels there is more of a rift in his personality than other people have	• Daren't sleep in case he turns into Hyde

How do I structure my ideas?

Make a **plan** for **paragraphs**.* Decide the order for your points:

● Paragraph 1: *Go straight into your first point: Jekyll has felt he has two warring parts since his youth.*

● Paragraph 2: *His distress was enough to lead him to a terrible experiment, but it made things worse.*

● Paragraph 3: *Stevenson shows Jekyll laid low by illness and distress, unable to associate with his friends or discuss his problems.*

● Paragraph 4: *By his own account, Jekyll suffers terribly and in ways no one else has done; he is the 'chief of sufferers'.*

● Paragraph 5: *There is no way out of his torment except death, or becoming Hyde forever.*

How do I write effectively?

Write **clear**, **analytical** paragraphs and **embed** your evidence well. For example:

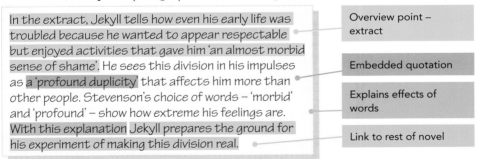

In the extract, Jekyll tells how even his early life was troubled because he wanted to appear respectable but enjoyed activities that gave him 'an almost morbid sense of shame'. He sees this division in his impulses as a 'profound duplicity' that affects him more than other people. Stevenson's choice of words – 'morbid' and 'profound' – show how extreme his feelings are. With this explanation Jekyll prepares the ground for his experiment of making this division real.

Overview point – extract

Embedded quotation

Explains effects of words

Link to rest of novel

Now you try!

Re-read Question 3 on page 65 and plan your response in the same way.

* The plan above and the sample answers on pages 68 and 70 have five paragraphs, but you don't need to be limited to this if you have more points to include.

What does a Grade 5 answer look like?

Read the task again, then the sample answer below.

1. Starting with this extract, how does Stevenson present Jekyll as tormented individual?

   Write about:

   ● how Stevenson presents Jekyll in this extract

   ● how Stevenson presents Jekyll as tormented in the novel as a whole.

   [30 marks]

Stevenson lets Jekyll explain for himself how there were two warring parts to his personality even when he was young. He set himself high standards of behaviour because he wanted other people's respect. At the same time, he liked doing things he thought were shameful. This caused him problems and he feels that there is in him a 'deeper trench than in the majority of men' dividing his good and bad parts.

> **AO2** Embedded quotation supports point

Jekyll tries to avoid this distress by making his potion. He expects this will mean he can still do the things he enjoys, as that part of him can act alone, but that he can also remain respectable and well thought of. He stresses the pain he was in before the experiment, referring to the 'curse of mankind' and the 'agonized womb of consciousness'. These extreme images tell us how much he felt he was suffering.

> **AO2** Relevant quotations

Even before he tells us what has happened, Jekyll calls himself a 'shipwreck'. A shipwreck is beyond fixing. The metaphor helps explain earlier parts of the novel. Stevenson has already shown Jekyll suffering extreme states, which is typical of Gothic novels. Jekyll won't discuss his problems and he ignores his friends. He seems very ill and unhappy to Utterson. When Utterson and Enfield see Jekyll at the window, they leave in silence.

> **AO1** Link to rest of the novel, needs expanding

> **AO3** Link to context, but undeveloped

In his statement and when he talks to Utterson and writes to Lanyon earlier in the novel, Jekyll often stresses just how much he suffers. He says he is the 'chief of sufferers' and that he had no idea 'sufferings and terrors so unmanning' were possible. He's a bit of a drama queen. He was certain the divide between good and bad was worse in him than in other people, and then he's certain he suffers more than anyone else ever. Partly, this is Stevenson doing what is expected in a Gothic novel, as Gothic literature often deals with extreme emotions and experiences. It is essential to the novel, though. When we realise what is actually happening – he is turning into Hyde for good, with no choice – we understand why it's so horrendous.

— Paragraph 4

At the end, Jekyll falls into despair because there are no options. In this Stevenson really is showing us a man who is tormented. He brought this about himself, but Stevenson still makes us feel sympathy for him. He can only die or be Hyde forever, and Hyde will be hanged for murder. Suicide is the only way out. It is strange though that Jekyll doesn't just kill himself before turning into Hyde the last time.

— Paragraph 5

Check the skills

Re-read paragraphs four and five of this response and:

- highlight other **points** made;
- circle any reference to **context**;
- underline any places where the student has made an **interpretation**.

Now you try!

Look again at paragraph three (*'Even before he tells us …'*, etc.) and improve it by:

- Adding a **reference or quotation** from elsewhere in the book that shows him as a man in torment.
- **Explaining** why Utterson and Enfield leave in silence and what this tells us about Jekyll's condition.
- Linking Jekyll's despair and how Stevenson has shown him earlier in the novel.
- Improving the overall **style** by making sure your sentences **flow**; using connectives to **link** ideas.

What does a Grade 7+ answer look like?

Read the task again, then the sample answer below.

1. Starting with this extract, how does Stevenson present Jekyll as a tormented individual?

   Write about:
   - how Stevenson presents Jekyll in this extract
   - how Stevenson presents Jekyll as tormented in the novel as a whole.

Stevenson shows Jekyll has been troubled by the two warring parts of his personality since his youth. Jekyll craved the good opinion of others, to the extent of hiding behaviour he thought reflected badly on him. He recalls his 'imperious desire' to seem better than others, his language acknowledging he was arrogant, and set his standards too high. He claims the 'trench' that 'severed' good and evil was deeper in him than in others. This may be true, or might be evidence that he still feels that he is special.

AO1 Immediately locates source of Jekyll's distress

AO2 Relevant embedded quotation

AO2 Analysis of language

Jekyll's distress led him to look for a way to separate the parts of himself. He turned to the new science of pharmacology. Stevenson could exploit this freely, as in the nineteenth century it was uncharted territory. Jekyll developed his potion to deal with a situation he frames in terms of suffering. He wanted to calm the 'perennial war' within him, so that 'life would be relieved of all that was unbearable'. The result was the unfixable 'shipwreck' of his reason.

AO1 Original interpretation

AO3 Context securely addressed

AO2 Successful embedded apt quotation

Jekyll's statement describes his suffering, but Stevenson has already shown it through the actions and words of Jekyll and others. We see Jekyll afraid, unable to confide in or see his friends, a physical and emotional wreck confined to his house. After he has lost control of the transformation process, he says he is the 'chief of sufferers', facing 'suffering and terrors so unmanning' he never imagined possible. Just the look on his face at the window leaves Utterson and Enfield horrified, able only to mutter '"God forgive us."'

AO1 Skilful link to early parts of the novel

AO1 Sound demonstration of point

In his statement Jekyll struggles to express the depth of his agony. Stevenson uses vivid, often horrifying, images to try to get across the extremity of his suffering. Unlike the other characters, who are repelled by and shun the diabolical Hyde, he is more than trapped with him: Hyde is 'closer than an eye' and 'caged' in his flesh. He recognises this 'demon' as not just his own but himself. He has, ironically, nowhere to hide from Hyde.

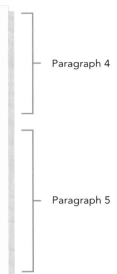

Paragraph 4

Jekyll considers himself special, and his suffering unparalleled, but only his situation is unique. Stevenson uses the novel to explore interesting universal questions about the dual nature of man, the dangers of science, and the nature of good and evil. He frames it as a Gothic novel, a genre concerned with the bizarre, the mysterious and extreme emotions and experiences. The lesson Jekyll learns, though, extends the horror beyond Jekyll's extraordinary situation. He concludes that the 'doom and burden' of our life is inescapable and trying to avoid it brings it back with 'more unfamiliar and more awful pressure'.

Paragraph 5

Check the skills

Re-read paragraphs four and five of this response and:

- identify any particularly **fluent** or **well-expressed** ideas;
- find any further references to **context**;
- highlight any places where the student has shown **deeper insight** and offered **original** or particularly **thoughtful** ideas or made interesting **links**.

Now you try!

Now, using the plan you made for Question 3 on page 67, write a full response. Here's a reminder of the question:

3. 'Stevenson presents much of the novel from Utterson's point of view, though not in his voice. Utterson's character is well suited to this role.' Starting with this extract, explore how far you agree with this opinion.

   Write about:

   - how Stevenson presents Utterson in this extract
   - how Stevenson's presentation of Utterson in the novel as a whole suits his role.

- Try to match your answer to the High Level objectives on page 63.

Read these exam-style theme questions

Read this extract from Chapter 9 in which Lanyon describes Hyde mixing the potion. Then answer the question that follows.

> He thanked me with a smiling nod, measured out a few minims of the red tincture and added one of the powders. The mixture, which was at first of a reddish hue, began, in proportion as the crystals melted, to brighten in colour, to effervesce audibly, and to throw off small fumes of vapour. Suddenly and
> 5 at the same moment, the ebullition ceased and the compound changed to a dark purple, which faded again more slowly to a watery green. My visitor, who had watched these metamorphoses with a keen eye, smiled, set down the glass upon the table, and then turned and looked upon me with an air of scrutiny.
> 'And now,' said he, 'to settle what remains. Will you be wise? will you be
> 10 guided? will you suffer me to take this glass in my hand and to go forth from your house without further parley? or has the greed of curiosity too much command of you? Think before you answer, for it shall be done as you decide. As you decide, you shall be left as you were before, and neither richer nor wiser, unless the sense of service rendered to a man in mortal distress may
> 15 be counted as a kind of riches of the soul. Or, if you shall so prefer to choose, a new province of knowledge and new avenues to fame and power shall be laid open to you, here, in this room, upon the instant; and your sight shall be blasted by a prodigy to stagger the unbelief of Satan.'
> 'Sir,' said I, affecting a coolness that I was far from truly possessing, 'you
> 20 speak enigmas, and you will perhaps not wonder that I hear you with no very strong impression of belief. But I have gone too far in the way of inexplicable services to pause before I see the end.'
> 'It is well,' replied my visitor. 'Lanyon, you remember your vows: what follows is under the seal of our profession. And now, you who have so long
> 25 been bound to the most narrow and material views, you who have denied the virtue of transcendental medicine, you who have derided your superiors – behold!'

4. Starting with this extract, explore how Stevenson presents science.

   Write about:
   - how Stevenson presents science in this extract
   - how Stevenson presents science in the novel as a whole.

   [30 marks]

Read this extract from Chapter 10 in which Jekyll is explaining what has happened. Then answer the question that follows.

> With every day, and from both sides of my intelligence, the moral and the intellectual, I thus drew steadily nearer to that truth, by whose partial discovery I have been doomed to such a dreadful shipwreck: that man is not truly one, but truly two. I say two, because the state of my own knowledge
> 5 does not pass beyond that point. Others will follow, others will outstrip me on the same lines; and I hazard the guess that man will be ultimately known for a mere polity of multifarious, incongruous and independent denizens. I for my part, from the nature of my life, advanced infallibly in one direction and in one direction only. It was on the moral side, and in my own person,
> 10 that I learned to recognize the thorough and primitive duality of man; I saw that, of the two natures that contended in the field of my consciousness, even if I could rightly be said to be either, it was only because I was radically both; and from an early date, even before the course of my scientific discoveries had begun to suggest the most naked possibility of such a miracle, I had learned to
> 15 dwell with pleasure, as a beloved daydream, on the thought of the separation of these elements. If each, I told myself, could but be housed in separate identities, life would be relieved of all that was unbearable; the unjust might go his way, delivered from the aspirations and remorse of his more upright twin; and the just could walk steadfastly and securely on his upward path,
> 20 doing the good things in which he found his pleasure, and no longer exposed to disgrace and penitence by the hands of this extraneous evil. It was the curse of mankind that these incongruous faggots were thus bound together – that in the agonised womb of consciousness, these polar twins should be continuously struggling. How, then, were they dissociated?

5. Starting with this extract, how does Stevenson present the duality of human nature?

Write about:

- how Stevenson presents the duality of human nature in this extract
- how Stevenson presents the duality of human nature in the novel as a whole.

[30 marks]

Five key stages to follow

1. **Read** the **question**; **highlight** key words.
2. **Read** the **extract** with the **key words** from the **question** in mind.
3. Quickly **generate ideas** for your response.
4. **Plan** for paragraphs.
5. **Write** your response; **check it** against your plan as you progress.

What do I focus on?

Highlight the **key words**:

> 4. Starting with this extract, explore how Stevenson presents science.
> Write about:
> - how Stevenson presents science in this extract
> - how Stevenson presents science in the novel as a whole.

What do they tell you? Focus on both extract and whole text; explain what specific methods Stevenson uses; stick to the presentation of science as the main topic.

How should I read the passage?

- Check for any immediate links to the question (e.g. Lanyon gives a detailed account of how the chemicals react).
- Look for any evidence/quotations you could highlight (e.g. calling scientific interest the **'greed of curiosity'**).

How do I get my ideas?

Note your ideas in a spider diagram or list them in a table:

The extract

The novel as a whole

Detailed account of chemical reaction

Science as dangerous – Hyde warns Lanyon's 'sight will be blasted'

Not really precise as we don't know the ingredients

Science

Lanyon and Jekyll have different attitudes to science

The extract	The novel as a whole
• Hyde warns against scientific curiosity	• Lanyon has a traditional attitude to science
• Lanyon is committed to scientific enquiry	• Jekyll's science is unorthodox and 'transcendental'

HOW do I structure my ideas?

Make a **plan** for **paragraphs**.* Decide the order for your points:

- Paragraph 1: *Go straight into your first point: Science is central to the novel.*
- Paragraph 2: *Lanyon has a traditional approach to science, which Jekyll considers narrow-minded.*
- Paragraph 3: *Jekyll calls his unusual science 'transcendental'.*
- Paragraph 4: *Stevenson reflects Victorian concerns about science.*
- Paragraph 5: *Science is shown as dangerous in leading Jekyll to his doom.*

HOW do I write effectively?

Write **clear**, **analytical** paragraphs and **embed** your evidence fluently. For example:

> Here, Stevenson presents contrasting approaches to scientific enquiry. Lanyon is committed to finding out what he can, and recording it carefully— the conventional way to do science. Hyde warns he doesn't watch, warning him against the dangers of science but tempts him with 'a new province of knowledge'. The word 'province', an area of land, stresses the link with exploration. These two views are central to Stevenson's presentation of science, which investigates questions of interest and urgency in the nineteenth century.

- Overview point – extract
- Stevenson's technique introduced
- Quotation embedded in the sentence
- Link to rest of novel
- Reference to context

Now you try!

Re-read Question 5 on page 73 and plan your response in the same way.

---

* The plan above and the sample answers on pages 76 and 78 have five paragraphs, but you don't need to be limited to this if you have more points to include (and time to write them!).

What does a Grade 5 answer look like?

Read the task again, then the sample answer below.

4. Starting with this extract, explore how Stevenson presents science.
   Write about:
   ● how Stevenson presents science in this extract
   ● how Stevenson presents science in the novel as a whole.

[30 marks]

Science is central to the novel as it's through science that Jekyll makes his potion and separates the parts of himself. Stevenson shows different attitudes towards science in Jekyll and Lanyon, and uses Jekyll's experiment to write about the dangers of science. Here, Lanyon gives a detailed account of Hyde mixing the potion. He lists the 'metamorphoses' (changes) in the mixture. Stevenson uses a scientific term to stress that Lanyon is a real, everyday scientist. Stevenson first studied engineering so knew about proper scientific language.

AO1 Clear topic statement

AO2 Further explores topic

AO2 Explains term

AO2 Explains effect of word choice

AO3 Attempt to draw in context, not linked

Lanyon has a traditional approach to science. He reports the external details of scientific processes: Hyde mixing the potion and how seeing Hyde affects Lanyon's own physical state. His account in the extract is calm and measured, just like a scientist reporting an experiment. By contrast, Hyde's account is an emotional outburst, though he is only asking if Lanyon wants to watch the rest of the experiment.

AO2 True, but point not expanded

Jekyll has a very different attitude to science. He is interested in the mind or spirit and how to split it from the body. He calls it 'transcendental medicine'. Lanyon is interested only in the body. Because he is appearing as Hyde here, Jekyll doesn't need to be polite. He is rude about Lanyon's views and accuses Lanyon of having 'derided your superiors'. Hyde can say what Jekyll really thinks and would like to say, but can't say as Jekyll. The difference in their views is really highlighted in this passage where they come face to face.

AO1 Clear contrast; needs supporting quotation

AO1 Good interpretation

There were many changes going on in science in the Victorian period, and Stevenson is dealing with questions that would have interested his readers. Pharmacology was a new science. It deals with how chemicals affect the body, like Jekyll's experiment. The theory of evolution made people think about human nature and what makes humans different from animals. Stevenson likens Hyde to an animal. He leaps 'like a monkey', makes a screech of 'mere animal terror' on the last night and Jekyll calls the bad part of him an 'animal within me'.

Paragraph 4

Stevenson's examination of science in the novel seems to come to the conclusion that it's dangerous. Jekyll faces the 'shipwreck' of his reason because of his experiment. He finds out that separating the parts of himself is deadly dangerous. It's not just being experimental that is dangerous, though, as Lanyon dies as well. He had been too committed to his own ideas and can't get over them being wrong. Science seems to be quite a risky pastime.

Paragraph 5

Check the skills

Re-read paragraphs four and five of this response and:

● highlight other **points** made;

● circle any reference to **context**;

● underline any places where the student has made an **interpretation**.

Now you try!

Look again at paragraph three ('*Jekyll has a very different attitude …*') and improve it by:

● Adding at least one **reference or quotation** about Jekyll or Lanyon from earlier in the book to demonstrate how their views differ.

● **Explaining** what Hyde means when he accuses Lanyon of having **'derided your superiors'**.

● Ending with a **summary point** about the importance of the difference in the views of Lanyon and Jekyll for the novel as a whole.

● Improving the overall **style** by making sure your sentences **flow**; using connectives to **link** ideas.

What does a Grade 7+ answer look like?

Read the task again, then the sample answer below.

4. Starting with this extract, explore how Stevenson presents science.
   Write about:
   - how Stevenson presents science in this extract
   - how Stevenson presents science in the novel as a whole.

[30 marks]

In the extract, Stevenson brings together the two characters he uses to explore the theme of science in the novel: Lanyon and Jekyll (here in the form of Hyde). The first paragraph, told in Lanyon's voice, represents Lanyon's own practical, evidence-based approach to science. The second, told in Hyde's voice, presents the wilder claims of Jekyll and his wide-ranging approach to 'transcendental' science. The rest of the novel explores the contrast between these approaches and the wider issue of the dangers or benefits of science.

AO1 Clear statement of idea

AO1 Indicates direction of argument clearly

Lanyon's approach to science is reflected in his account of the potion as Hyde mixes it. He itemizes the changes in the mixture, using scientific terms such as 'effervesce', 'ebullition' and 'metamorphoses'. The prose is measured and calm, descriptive and precise, in the way we would expect a scientist to record a reaction he or she watched. Similarly, Lanyon notes the effect Hyde has on his own physical state with clinical accuracy, noting his own emotions as though he were observing a patient. Stevenson portrays him as a typical conventional scientist.

AO2 Well-chosen evidence showing effect of word choice

AO2 Excellent account of effect of language

AO1 Skilful link between paragraphs

Jekyll, on the other hand, considers Lanyon's view of science 'most narrow and material', and Lanyon a 'hide-bound pedant'. Jekyll's research 'led wholly towards the mystic and the transcendental'. In making a potion to affect his personality or spirit, Stevenson shows him experimenting in the new science of pharmacology, just taking off in the nineteenth century. Some new developments were widely distrusted — Stevenson taps into this for Lanyon's dismissal of Jekyll's work as 'unscientific balderdash'.

AO2 Embedded quotations used to make a point

AO3 Good link to context

AO2 Further development of point, linking into text

Hyde refers to the 'greed of curiosity' which might lead Lanyon to watch Hyde take the potion. Greed is a sin, and in Hyde's sneering speech the 'greed of curiosity' comes across as a bad thing. This raises a larger question. Progress in science was calling established beliefs into question. Darwin's theory of evolution challenged what it means to be human, and cast doubt on the biblical story of creation — which itself deals with the dangers of knowledge.

Paragraph 4

Jekyll's downfall comes from going too far, overstepping the limits of safe or bearable knowledge. This reflects the threat science seemed to pose in Stevenson's time. Lanyon later sums up the danger: 'if we knew all, we should be more glad to get away'. Yet Lanyon is killed by the shock of having his secure, 'narrow' view overturned. Both men are driven by the same 'greed' and both come to grief. We, too, are driven by the 'greed of curiosity' to read on and discover the true horror of Jekyll's situation. Stevenson shows the desire for knowledge, represented by science, as both dangerous and compelling.

Paragraph 5

Check the skills

Re-read paragraphs four and five of this response and:

- identify any particularly **fluent** or **well-expressed** ideas;
- find any further references to **context**;
- highlight any places where the student has shown **deeper insight** and offered **original** or particularly **thoughtful** ideas or made interesting **links**.

Now you try!

Now, using the plan you made for Question 5 on page 75, write a full response. Here's a reminder of the question:

5. Starting with this extract, how does Stevenson present the duality of human nature?

Write about:

- how Stevenson presents the duality of human nature in this extract
- how Stevenson presents the duality of human nature in the novel as a whole.

- Try to match your answer to the High Level objectives on page 63.

Now you try!

Practise applying the skills you have learned to these two new questions.

- Note down key points from the extract.
- Select the key quotations you want to use from the extract.
- Repeat the process with other ideas from the novel as a whole.
- Write your answer.
- Look at the suggested list of key points you could have made for each question in the **Answers** (page 88).

Read this extract from Chapter 6 in which Utterson has written to Jekyll to ask why he has fallen out with Lanyon, and he reads Jekyll's reply. Then answer the question that follows.

> The quarrel with Lanyon was incurable. 'I do not blame our old friend,' Jekyll wrote, 'but I share his view that we must never meet. I mean from henceforth to lead a life of extreme seclusion; you must not be surprised, nor must you doubt my friendship, if my door is often shut even to you. You must
> 5   suffer me to go my own dark way. I have brought on myself a punishment and a danger that I cannot name. If I am the chief of sinners, I am the chief of sufferers also. I could not think that this earth contained a place for sufferings and terrors so unmanning; and you can do but one thing, Utterson, to lighten this destiny, and that is to respect my silence.' Utterson was amazed; the dark
> 10   influence of Hyde had been withdrawn, the doctor had returned to his old tasks and amities; a week ago, the prospect had smiled with every promise of a cheerful and an honoured age; and now in a moment, friendship, and peace of mind, and the whole tenor of his life were wrecked. So great and unprepared a change pointed to madness; but in view of Lanyon's manner and words, there
> 15   must lie for it some deeper ground.

6. Starting with this extract, explore how Stevenson presents the relationship between Utterson and Jekyll.

Write about:

- how Stevenson presents the relationship between Utterson and Jekyll in this extract
- how Stevenson presents the relationship between Utterson and Jekyll in the novel as a whole.

[30 marks]

Read this extract from Chapter 10 in which Jekyll describes first turning into Hyde and his recognition of Hyde's evil. Then answer the question that follows.

> I must here speak by theory alone, saying not that which I know, but that which I suppose to be most probable. The evil side of my nature, to which I had now transferred the stamping efficacy, was less robust and less developed than the good which I had just deposed. Again, in the course of my life, which
> 5 had been, after all, nine tenths a life of effort, virtue and control, it had been much less exercised and much less exhausted. And hence, as I think, it came about that Edward Hyde was so much smaller, slighter and younger than Henry Jekyll. Even as good shone upon the countenance of the one, evil was written broadly and plainly on the face of the other. Evil besides (which I must
> 10 still believe to be the lethal side of man) had left on that body an imprint of deformity and decay. And yet when I looked upon that ugly idol in the glass, I was conscious of no repugnance, rather of a leap of welcome. This, too, was myself. It seemed natural and human. In my eyes it bore a livelier image of the spirit, it seemed more express and single, than the imperfect and divided
> 15 countenance, I had been hitherto accustomed to call mine. And in so far I was doubtless right. I have observed that when I wore the semblance of Edward Hyde, none could come near to me at first without a visible misgiving of the flesh. This, as I take it, was because all human beings, as we meet them, are commingled out of good and evil: and Edward Hyde, alone in the ranks of
> 20 mankind, was pure evil.

7. Starting with this extract, consider how Stevenson explores good and evil through Jekyll and Hyde.

Write about:

- how Stevenson presents good and evil in this extract
- how Stevenson presents good and evil elsewhere in the novel.

[30 marks]

GLOSSARY

Literary terms	Explanation
allegory	a narrative, short story, poem or other work in which the characters or events are symbols that stand for ideas about life or society
clause	a special phrase whose head is a verb. A clause can be a complete sentence
climax	the high point of a play, act or story
colloquial	the everyday speech used by people in ordinary situations
dialogue	speech and conversation between characters
epistolary	a novel or story written as series of letters
Gothic	in literature a style that includes horror, the supernatural, romance and death
imagery	descriptive language that uses images to make actions, objects and characters more vivid in the reader's mind
irony	deliberately saying one thing when you mean another, usually in a humorous, sarcastic or sometimes thoughtful way
metaphor	when one thing is used to describe another to create a striking or unusual image
monologue	speech or thoughts of a single character, not interacting with others
mood	the tone or atmosphere created by an artistic work
narrative	the construction of the storyline in a novel or story from beginning through middle to end, though how it is told varies
personification	the treatment or description of an object or idea as though they were human with human feelings and attributes
phrase	a group of words that work together to create a small unit of sense
pirate copy	unauthorised and illegal copy of a book produced without the author's or publisher's permission, and without paying them
pitch	how high or low a sound is
plot twist	an unexpected or unpredictable turn of events in the larger series of events that make up the plot of a story
protagonist	the main character
repetition	repeated words or patterns
rhetorical question	aa question sked for effect rather than for an answer
rhythm	sound pattern of strong and weak 'beats' made by language spoken aloud
sermon	a religious text usually delivered aloud like a lecture, which develops an argument about a point of religious belief or part of the Bible
shilling shocker	cheap book presenting a sensationalist story, produced in large numbers for mass market sales in the nineteenth century
simile	when one thing is compared directly with another using 'like' or 'as'
symbol	something that represents something else, sometimes with meanings that are widely known (e.g. a dove as a symbol of peace)
theme	an idea running through a work of literature or art
voice	All characters can have a voice, and the author has a voice, which can be a construct

ANSWERS

Note that the sample paragraphs given here provide only one possible approach to each task. Many other approaches would also be valid and appropriate.

PLOT AND STRUCTURE

Chapters 1-3 – Now you try! (page 7)
Another character introduced in the opening chapters is Hyde. We first see him through Enfield's account of an episode in which Hyde 'trampled calmly over the child's body and left her screaming on the ground'. His calmness seems inhuman and makes the response of others to him understandable. It also arouses our curiosity about him. Mystery will be an important aspect of the depiction of Hyde, so this is appropriate.

Chapters 4-6 – Now you try! (page 9)
Another feature of the Gothic is explored in Jekyll's account of his misery. He has 'brought on myself a punishment and a danger that I cannot name'. He emphasises the horrific and extreme nature of what he suffers, building a sense of mystery by withholding details. The extremes of experience, violent emotion and mystery are all common concerns of Gothic novels.

Chapters 7-8 – Now you try! (page 11)
Stevenson uses uncertainty about who or what is in the cabinet to raise the tension. Poole and Utterson hear a 'dismal screech, as of mere animal terror' from the cabinet. The reference to 'animal terror' suggests it is not Jekyll. Hyde has been associated with beasts, so this signals that it might be Hyde. We, like the characters, are eager to find out.

Chapter 9 – Now you try! (page 13)
Jekyll and Lanyon have different ideas about science. When Hyde speaks to Lanyon, he taunts Lanyon by saying he has 'long been bound to the most narrow and material views'. This characterises Lanyon's view of science: it is the conventional view that relies on physical evidence and proof. It is at odds with Jekyll's more abstract and, in Lanyon's view, 'fanciful' interests.

Chapter 10 – Now you try! (page 15)
The theme of good and evil is further developed in Chapter 10. This is explored in the division of Jekyll into his normal, good, self and his evil alter ego, Hyde. Jekyll believes that good and evil 'divide and compound man's dual nature': they both split us and also combine to make a single human character.

Form and structure – Now you try! (page 17)
Stevenson borrows elements from the Gothic novel. Events are often half-seen, and there are gaps, as when 'the maid fainted. It was two o'clock when she came to herself'. Action takes place just out of sight, with scenes ending just before or starting just after an event, or showing only part of it. This creates a sense of mystery and unease.

Quick revision – Quick quiz (pages 18-19)
1. They pass the door Hyde used. 2. £100. 3. He is named in Jekyll's will. 4. That Hyde is blackmailing Jekyll. 5. Sir Danvers Carew. 6. Hyde told him his address in Chapter 1. 7. A cane. 8. Because Guest is an expert at reading character from handwriting. 9. He is turning into Hyde. 10. An axe and a poker. 11. Weeping, and pacing footsteps. 12. He has taken poison. 13. A drawer of chemicals. 14. That Jekyll has gone mad or has a brain disease. 15. To watch or not to watch what will happen. 16. He awoke as Hyde, having not taken the potion. 17. After the murder of Carew. 18. Jekyll had run out of the potion and could not make more. 19. An impurity in one of the chemicals was a necessary ingredient. 20. Two: the maid who witnesses the murder and Hyde's landlady.

Quick revision – Power paragraphs (page 19)
1. The story is told by an anonymous narrator from Utterson's point of view. This limits the action to scenes that Utterson sees, so Stevenson uses other narrators speaking or writing to Utterson. Enfield tells Utterson about Hyde trampling the child, and both Lanyon and Jekyll leave documents for him. Utterson's role ends when he **'trudged back to his office to read the two narratives in which this mystery was now to be explained'.**

2. The letter explains why Lanyon and Jekyll have fallen out, who Hyde is, and how he is connected with Jekyll. Utterson knew Jekyll and Lanyon fell out over science, but he could not have guessed how far it went. The final rift with Jekyll comes after Lanyon sees **'a prodigy to stagger the unbelief of Satan'**: the transformation of Hyde into Jekyll. Though the link between Jekyll and Hyde is revealed, a lot is still unexplained.

Quick revision – Exam practice (page 19)
1.
- Builds on two aspects of Utterson's character: that he is a lawyer, and that he is a loyal friend
- Assumes Hyde is blackmailing Jekyll
- Sort of situation familiar from legal life
- Supports description of him as a loyal friend — wants to help Jekyll
- 'some old sin, the cancer of some concealed disgrace'

2.
- Utterson gives a down-to-earth explanation
- Looks as if it might be a crime story
- Stevenson sets us off in the wrong direction, preparing to build mystery and surprise
- '"Ay, it must be that"'

SETTING AND CONTEXT

Victorian London and the Gothic tradition – Now you try! (page 21)

Stevenson uses reputation to explain Jekyll's motives making his potion. He is 'fond of the respect of the wise and the good among my fellow-men', and keen to hide behaviour he is ashamed of. Keeping up good appearances in public was very important at the time, and often bad behaviour was hidden. Hyde provides Jekyll with the perfect way to hide his actions.

Science – Now you try! (page 23)

Stevenson shows the dangerous appeal of knowledge in Jekyll's experiment. Seeking forbidden knowledge led to the Fall of Man in the Bible, and damned the fictional character Faust in a well-known story. For Jekyll, too, 'the temptation of a discovery so singular and profound, at last overcame the suggestions of alarm'. Science reveals to him things that should not be known, and leads to his downfall and death.

Quick revision – Quick questions (page 25)

1. Smog was a mix of fog and smoke. 2. Victorian London was plagued by social inequality and crime. 3. Gothic literature often has a dark, spooky setting. 4. Graphology and physiognomy both feature in the novel. 5. Doctors often held surgeries in their own houses. 6. Servants looked after the houses of richer people. 7. Charles Darwin. 8. Stevenson was addicted to cocaine. 9. *Frankenstein* by Mary Shelley. 10. The rich behaved respectably in public but often behaved badly in private.

Quick revision – Power paragraphs (page 25)

Answers will vary.

CHARACTERS

Dr Jekyll in Chapters 1–7 – Now you try! (page 27)

Lanyon surprises Utterson with his view of Jekyll. They are old friends, but says they have fallen out because '"Henry Jekyll became too fanciful for me. He began to go wrong, wrong in mind"'. Later, the rift has become worse and Lanyon considers Jekyll dead to him. Stevenson uses Lanyon's strongly expressed views to increase the mystery around Jekyll.

Dr Jekyll in Chapters 8–10 – Now you try! (page 29)

Stevenson offers insight into Jekyll's self-satisfaction through the words he gives him. When Jekyll says 'I smiled, comparing myself with other men, comparing my active good-will with the lazy cruelty of their neglect' it suggests that he thinks he is better than most people. This attitude is clear in his dangerous experiment: he seems to think the usual rules of human behaviour don't apply to him.

Mr Hyde – Now you try! (page 31)

Jekyll is the only character who truly knows Hyde. He explains Hyde's character from the inside. When he first changes into Hyde he describes being aware that he was 'more wicked, tenfold more wicked' than his normal self. He recognises that this is as much a part of him as the respectable Jekyll, although he is unwilling to accept responsibility for Hyde's terrible actions.

Mr Utterson – Now you try! (page 33)

Utterson is a friend of Dr Jekyll and Dr Lanyon. Stevenson shows him interacting with them, trying to get to the root of their differences and supporting them. The narrator also reports that 'his affections, like ivy, were the growth of time, they implied no aptness in the object'. This tells us that Utterson does not choose friends carefully but becomes close to people he spends time with.

Dr Lanyon – Now you try! (page 35)

Lanyon and Jekyll are old friends, but Lanyon has fallen out with him because he doesn't share Jekyll's view of science. They are still close enough to dine together (Chapter 6) and for him to collect chemicals from Jekyll's laboratory, though he fears Jekyll is mad. After the transformation and hearing Jekyll's account, though, he cuts all ties with Jekyll, referring to him as 'one whom I regard as dead'.

Poole and Mr Enfield – Now you try! (page 37)

Mr Enfield's role in the novel relies on his relationship with Utterson. He tells the story of how he runs after Hyde, presenting himself as bold and brave: he 'gave a view halloa, took to my heels, collared my gentleman, and brought him back'. Catching Hyde sets the rest of the action in motion.

Minor characters – Now you try! (page 39)

Mr Guest is Utterson's head clerk. While he is Utterson's social inferior, he is intellectual enough for Utterson to chat and drink wine with. His role relies on Utterson trusting him to look at Hyde's letter and stay quiet about it. Utterson needs and trusts Guest's expertise in interpreting handwriting, a pseudo-science that was taken seriously in Victorian England.

Quick revision – Quick quiz (pages 40–41)

1. Sir Danvers Carew. 2. Jekyll wants to appear extremely respectable. 3. Lanyon thinks Jekyll has gone mad. 4. Utterson. 5. Lanyon is a medical doctor. 6. Utterson walks with his cousin, Mr Enfield. 7. Hyde wears Jekyll's clothes. They are too large and look ridiculous. 8. Utterson is Jekyll's lawyer. 9. He hopes it will be good for his career if he finds the murderer. 10. She is silent and unscrupulous. 11. Sir Danvers Carew. 12. He thinks he is too narrow-minded and materialistic. 13. Poole. 14. Utterson thinks Hyde is blackmailing Jekyll. 15. Guest is expert at reading character in handwriting. 16. Sir Danvers Carew. 17. Lanyon has known Jekyll for a long time. 18. What he has seen has so shocked Lanyon that it has made him ill. 19. Utterson denies himself simple pleasures. 20. Jekyll could kill Hyde by killing himself.

Quick revision – Power paragraphs (page 41)

1. All characters except Jekyll respond instinctively to Hyde with repulsion. They all feel there is 'something abnormal and misbegotten in the very essence of the creature', but no one can quite identify what it is. He seems to be somehow deformed or abnormal, but not in a way that can be described. Enfield remarks that even the doctor attending the trampled child seemed to want to kill him. The maid 'had conceived a dislike' for Hyde. Lanyon, observing his own reaction as a doctor, decides there is something not just unpleasant but deeply unnatural about Hyde. The only person who is not repulsed by Hyde is Jekyll. He is rather thrilled by Hyde's energy and passion for pleasure.

2. Stevenson uses Enfield to introduce Mr Hyde. Enfield tells Utterson how he saw Hyde trample a small child, and took the initiative to catch him — 'I gave a view halloa, took to my heels, collared my gentleman, and brought him back'. This starts the action, rousing Utterson's curiosity about Hyde. Stevenson uses Enfield again later as he goes with Utterson into Jekyll's courtyard and they see the horror that crosses Jekyll's face before he changes into Hyde.

Quick revision – Exam practice (page 41)

1.
- Poole's social status makes it hard for him to challenge Utterson
- His 'mottled palor' shows his annoyance
- Uses rhetorical questions to emphasise his certainty and how well he knows Jekyll
- 'do you think I do not know my master …?'

2.
- Poole knows where Jekyll's head comes to on the door – intimate detail conveys affection
- Describes Jekyll as 'a tall, fine build of a man'
- Describes Hyde as 'it' and 'that thing' – language makes Hyde an object, not human

THEMES

Duality – Now you try! (page 43)

Stevenson demonstrates the duality of human nature by splitting Jekyll into two characters. Jekyll eventually recognises that it is 'the curse of mankind that these incongruous faggots were thus bound together'. Controlling the pleasure-seeking part of his personality, is the normal state of being human. His attempt to separate the parts of himself is fatal.

Good and evil – Now you try! (page 45)

Stevenson shows that all people are a mix of good and evil. Jekyll discovers through his fatal experiment that 'all human beings, as we meet them, are commingled out of good and evil'. While his evil aspect remained trapped within him, he could keep it under control, and that is how we all live, by 'balancing instincts'.

Science – Now you try! (page 47)

Lanyon is a traditional scientist, focused on testable evidence. He watches Hyde take the potion because as a scientist he is curious and feels that he has 'gone too far in the way of inexplicable services to pause before I see the end'. This mix of curiosity and commitment to practical science leads to his death, as he cannot stand the challenge to his scientific view.

The law – Now you try! (page 49)

Stevenson uses a legal document, Jekyll's will, to introduce the mystery about Hyde. Documents are a central motif, tempting Utterson 'to disregard the prohibition and dive at once to these mysteries' and ignore their legal status by reading them before the deaths of Jekyll and Lanyon. These documents uncover the story behind the narrative and explain everything, including Hyde's crimes.

Reputation and secrecy – Now you try! (page 51)

The novel is built around secrecy, mystery and things that cannot be said. It follows Utterson trying to discover the secret Jekyll will not reveal: who Hyde is. Even when the central mystery is uncovered, others remain. Stevenson suggests that some secrets cannot be told as language fails; Jekyll faces 'a punishment and a danger that I cannot name' and Lanyon does not record the terrible things Jekyll told him.

Friendship – Now you try! (page 53)

Stevenson portrays a friendship broken by a strong difference of opinion between Lanyon and Jekyll. Even so, Jekyll turns to Lanyon, claiming 'my life, my honour, my reason, are all at your mercy', and Lanyon helps him. Jekyll recalls no 'break in our affection', but Hyde is vicious in his criticism of Lanyon. This reflects Jekyll's true fury at Lanyon's dismissal of his ideas.

Quick revision – Quick quiz (pages 54–55)

1. Utterson and Inspector Newcomen. 2. He is an expert in graphology – reading character from handwriting. 3. He is trying to protect his reputation. 4. They have fallen out over Jekyll's scientific interests. 5. The two walk in silence and don't appear to engage with each other. 6. He pays the money to avoid a scene. 7. She is unscrupulous and will keep his evil deeds secret. 8. He is friends with people he has known a long time. 9. Lanyon and Jekyll. 10. Hyde. 11. Sir Danvers Carew. 12. Human beings probably have more than two contrasting aspects. 13. He wants to hide behaviour he considers **'immoderate'** and slightly shameful. 14. Jekyll. 15. Utterson and Lanyon are Jekyll's oldest friends. 16. Utterson is Jekyll's lawyer and keeps his will. 17. The chemicals Poole brings each time don't work in the potion. 18. As a scientist, Lanyon is curious to see what will happen. 19. Hyde is unnatural because he is half a person, only one of mankind's dual aspects. 20. Utterson is afraid of **'the law and the law's officers'**.

ANSWERS

Quick revision – Power paragraphs (page 55)

1. Jekyll is very concerned to 'wear a more than commonly grave countenance before the public'. He hides pleasures he thinks of as 'immoderate' to protect his reputation. The tension that creates leads him to develop his potion so that he can still indulge his appetites. Once he does not have to keep his urges under control, they grow stronger, until eventually they take him over completely and he stays as Hyde.

2. Stevenson shows science leading to the deaths of Carew, Jekyll and Lanyon in different ways. Carew is murdered by Hyde, released by Jekyll's potion. Jekyll is a victim of his own experiment, as he has destroyed himself by splitting his personality. Even the practical and sceptical Lanyon is destroyed, as he can't stand the shock to his scientific certainty that Jekyll's experiment brings.

Quick revision – Exam practice (page 55)

1.
- Turning point in the novel as he turns without using the potion
- Giving up the potion means Jekyll is living only half of his nature
- Inevitably he starts to want pleasure again, as human nature is a mix of good and bad
- 'still cursed with my duality of purpose'

2.
- Too late to return to a normal person: has fatally disrupted his mind and body
- Prompted to separate dual parts of human nature to be good and bad separately so he could enjoy private pleasures and still be respectable
- Part of human condition to have good and bad/ spirit and body/appetites and reason in tension – not possible to split them and survive
- 'it was the curse of mankind that these incongruous faggots were thus bound together'

LANGUAGE

Imagery and vocabulary – Now you try! (page 57)

The novel is full of extreme emotions beyond readers' experiences. Stevenson uses language to make them more accessible, as when he uses a domestic image to describe Hyde as having 'a soul boiling with causeless hatreds'. The image of a pot boiling is familiar; we can imagine the chaotic, roiling motion of the dangerously hot water and transfer that sense to Hyde's mind.

Narrative style and voice – Now you try! (page 59)

Stevenson uses Poole's voice to tell us about his character and social status. Poole speaks much more simply than the other characters. He draws on folk wisdom when giving Utterson his view of Hyde's pacing, '"Ah, it's an ill-conscience that's such an enemy to rest!"' This shows him as a man of lower social status, less intellectual than the three main characters.

Quick revision – Quick questions (page 61)

1. The evening is tranquil and pleasant. 2. Jekyll. 3. Poole uses rhetorical questions to show Utterson he knows it was Hyde in the laboratory. 4. It makes Hyde sound less than human, like an object. 5. He shows that Utterson is of a higher social status than Poole. 6. Hyde. 7. Metaphor. 8. It sounds cosy and welcoming. 9. Simile. 10. To give a command without it sounding like one.

Quick revision – Power paragraphs (page 61)

Answers will vary.

EXAM PRACTICE

Planning your character response – Now you try! (page 67)

- Paragraph 1: Utterson is dull but kindly, tolerant and non-judgemental, and a professional lawyer, so he won't be quick to condemn other characters.
- Paragraph 2: He is often the last to stand by 'down-going men', so will be around for Jekyll until the end.
- Paragraph 3: His willingness to help others is borne out elsewhere in the novel: he tries to help Jekyll, takes Newcomen to Hyde's lodgings, and helps Poole on the last night. In this way Stevenson keeps him near the action.
- Paragraph 4: As he is friends with those he has known a long time, he has quite different friends and is linked to all parts of the story.
- Paragraph 5: Some characteristics seem to make him less well suited to his role. He jumps to wrong conclusions and acts on them, misleading us. This suits Stevenson's purpose in sustaining the mystery.

Grade 5 sample answer – Check the skills! (page 69)

- **Points:** Paragraph 4: Jekyll says he suffers terrible torments and thinks are worse for him than for other people. Stevenson sets high expectations of the horror that are not disappointed, though this is not very clearly expressed. Paragraph 5: Jekyll's torments can only be ended by death.
- **Context:** *this is Stevenson doing what is expected in a Gothic novel, as Gothic literature often deals with extreme emotions and experiences.* The answer relates Jekyll's experiences to the genre of Gothic literature.
- **Interpretations:** *He's a bit of a drama queen. He was certain the divide between good and bad was worse in him than in other people, and then he's certain he suffers more than anyone else ever.* The phrasing is too informal, but the points are valid.

Grade 5 sample answer – Now you try! (page 69)

Even before telling the rest of his story, Jekyll refers to the 'shipwreck' he has become: the metaphor tells us he has destroyed himself. It explains later parts of the novel in which Stevenson shows Jekyll suffering. Extreme emotional and mental states are characteristic of Gothic novels, but Jekyll's torment is shown convincingly through his behaviour. Jekyll refuses to discuss his problems or see his friends, and appears terribly ill and unhappy – signs of his despair. His look of 'abject terror and despair' at the window so horrifies

Utterson and Enfield they don't know what to say and leave in silence.

Grade 7+ sample answer – Check the skills! (page 71)

- **Points:** Jekyll struggles to articulate the depth of his agony. Stevenson uses vivid images to try to get across the extremity of his suffering. He recognizes the 'demon' Hyde as part of himself; he has, ironically, nowhere to hide from Hyde.
- **Context:** Stevenson frames the tale as a Gothic novel, a genre concerned with the borders of experience and extreme emotion.
- **Interpretations:** Jekyll considers himself special, and his suffering unparalleled; only his circumstances are unique. The lesson Jekyll learns about human nature, applies to all of us and extends the horror beyond Jekyll's situation

Grade 7+ sample answer – Now you try! (page 71)

AO1: The description of Utterson here suggests he will be reliable — a useful quality in someone who provides the viewpoint for telling the story. 'backward in sentiment; lean, long, dusty, dreary'

AO1: Utterson is good friends with the main characters, Lanyon and Jekyll, so has as much access to their thoughts and actions as possible.

AO1: Utterson jumps to conclusions and then acts as though they are correct, which seems to make him less qualified to provide the guiding point of view. 'Ay, it must be that; the ghost of some old sin'

AO1: Utterson sticks by friends in trouble and tries to help people, both qualities that will keep him engaged in the fates of Jekyll and Lanyon, and near the action as he helps Newcomen and Poole. 'the last reputable acquaintance and the last good influence in the lives of down-going men'

AO2: Utterson's language reflects his profession; he formulates logical ideas, even if they are wrong, as when he tells Poole his theory of why Jekyll is hiding. '"it is plain and natural, hangs well together and delivers us from all exorbitant alarms"'

AO2: Most of the story is told from Utterson's viewpoint, revealing things as he learns them and in his voice. 'some Jack-in-the-box of an old iniquity'

AO2: Stevenson uses our trust in Utterson's viewpoint to keep the real link between Jekyll and Hyde obscure, as we accept Utterson's mistaken assumptions.

AO2: Structurally, Stevenson builds mystery in the novel by having Utterson repeatedly express his confusion and what he does not know: 'putting his hand to his brow like a man in mental perplexity'

AO3: Utterson acts as a sort of hub in the novel, as other narratives, including documents, come to him. This is a common feature of Gothic novels.

AO3: Stevenson himself trained in the law, and his presentation of Utterson as both dry and dull and not as reliable as we might expect perhaps reflect his own experience of lawyers and trainee lawyers.

Planning your theme response – Now you try! (page 75)

- Paragraph 1: Go straight into your first point: Jekyll is painfully aware of the duality of human nature.

- Paragraph 2: Human nature combines a rational part and a part that follows basic appetites.
- Paragraph 3: It seems to Jekyll that separating the parts could allow him to live a better life.
- Paragraph 4: When freed from the conscious control of Jekyll, Hyde's evil quickly takes over.
- Paragraph 5: Stevenson shows that managing our conflicting urges is central to the human condition.

Grade 5 sample answer – Check the skills! (page 77)

- **Points:** Science is dangerous in more ways than one; it can be dangerous to be too experimental and **also** to be too closely tied to one set of ideas.
- **Context:** Many changes were going on in nineteenth-century science; Darwin developed the theory of evolution, and pharmacology.
- **Interpretation:** Stevenson's examination of science in the novel seems to come to the conclusion that it's dangerous. Lanyon had been too committed to his own ideas and can't get over them being wrong.

Grade 5 sample answer – Now you try! (page 77)

Jekyll's attitude towards science is very different. He calls it 'mystic and transcendental', but Lanyon calls it 'unscientific balderdash'. Jekyll is interested in the mind or spirit and how to split it from the body, while Lanyon is interested only in the body. As Hyde doesn't need to be polite to Lanyon, he can say what Jekyll thinks and would like to say. Hyde blasts Lanyon's views as 'narrow and material' (and accuses Lanyon of having 'derided your superiors'. This is means Jekyll believes he is far better than Lanyon. Their different views have led to Jekyll and Lanyon falling out.

Grade 7+ sample answer – Check the skills! (page 79)

- **Points**: Jekyll's downfall comes from going too far, overstepping the limits of safe or endurable knowledge. Stevenson shows the desire for knowledge, represented by science, as both dangerous and compelling.
- **Context:** Science was making rapid progress in the nineteenth century and calling established beliefs into question. Darwin's theory of evolution cast doubt on human nature itself, as well as on the biblical story of creation. This reflects the threat science seemed to pose to Stevenson's audience.
- **Interpretation:** Casts doubt on the biblical story of creation – which itself deals with the dangers of knowledge. We, too, are driven by the 'greed of curiosity' to read on and discover the true horror of Jekyll's situation.

Grade 7+ sample answer – Now you try! (page 79)

AO1: Jekyll is aware of two conflicting parts in his nature, which here he terms the 'unjust' and the 'just'.

AO1: Jekyll's aim in separating the two parts of himself is to escape 'all that was unbearable', and it seems that early in his experiment he might succeed.

AO1: Hyde grows in size and power; Stevenson shows in this way that if the 'unjust' part is not kept in check by reason it gets out of hand.

AO1: Human nature is necessarily made of two (or

more) parts, constantly in tension, and it's impossible to avoid the task of keeping them in balance. 'when the attempt is made to cast it off, it but returns upon us with more unfamiliar and more awful pressure'

AO2: The conflict between these two causes him pain, which comes across in the imagery Stevenson uses. 'agonised womb of consciousness' 'polar twins should be continuously struggling'

AO2: Stevenson uses language to associate Hyde with animals and with Satan, suggesting that simple desires and evil motivate him. 'the animal within me licking the chops of memory' 'Satan's signature upon a face'

AO2: The form of the narrative, split between narratorial points of view, mimics the lesson about human nature, split into different aspects of personality.

AO2: Stevenson gives Jekyll the task of trying to explain how integral Hyde is to his being. He at first uses literal language and speaks in the first person, but later resorts to imagery to get this across and speaks in the third person of himself (or himselves). 'This, too, was myself.' 'knit to him closer than a wife, closer than an eye; lay caged in his flesh'

AO3: Jekyll mentions that the dual nature of humankind 'lies at the root of religion', referring to the conflict between body and soul discussed in both religion and philosophy (e.g. Plato, Descartes – philosophers Victorian readers would know about).

AO3: As a gentleman in the nineteenth century, certain standards of behaviour would have been expected of Jekyll. It is the pressure of social respectability that drives him to try to hide the part of his nature he is ashamed of.

Practice questions – Question 6 (page 80)

AO1: Jekyll challenges the notion of friendship, an important theme, by asking Utterson to be his friend by not seeking to see him or speak to him. '"you can do but one thing, Utterson, to lighten this destiny, and that is to respect my silence"'

AO1: Utterson has both a professional and a personal relationship with Jekyll, as he is both his lawyer and his friend. This gives him unique access to Jekyll's situation (he keeps his will) and his state of mind.

AO1: Stevenson presents Utterson as a man who is often 'the last good influence in the lives of down-going' friends; this is demonstrated in his relationship with Jekyll.

AO1: On the final night, Utterson demonstrates his friendship by ignoring Jekyll's wishes when he breaks down the door to the cabinet in the hope of helping Jekyll.

AO2: The form of the conversation contrasts with its content: it's equally split between Jekyll's words and Utterson's reaction to them, but this doesn't reflect a balance of power. Jekyll is now dictating the terms of their friendship and Utterson has no say.

AO2: Stevenson shows us Jekyll through Utterson's eyes here, introduced by 'Utterson was amazed'. He then itemises the evidence as Utterson would present it himself.

AO2: Utterson's relationship with Jekyll is central to the novel. Utterson's concern for Jekyll drives him to investigate Hyde, and Stevenson uses Jekyll's statement, left for Utterson to read, to reveal the mystery.

AO2: When Jekyll says he is suffering 'a punishment and a danger that I cannot name', he is not just unwilling to talk to his friend. We realise later that literally there is no language to explain his trouble, as it is an entirely new experience.

AO3: Jekyll expresses his despair in extravagant terms characteristic of Gothic literature. 'I could not think that this earth contained a place for sufferings and terrors so unmanning'

AO3: Utterson first interprets Jekyll's behaviour as a sign of madness, which Lanyon had also done. Madness is a common theme in Gothic literature.

Practice questions – Question 7 (page 81)

AO1: Stevenson shows evil as ugly, and, in the form of Hyde, immediately repulsive to all normal people. But Jekyll is not repelled by Hyde, suggesting that we are immune to or tolerant of our own evil. The 'leap of welcome' Jekyll feels shows, too, the dangerous attractiveness of evil.

AO1: Although Hyde starts off small and weak, he grows much stronger during the novel. Stevenson shows through Hyde that bad behaviour quickly escalates when there is no attempt to control it.

AO1: Other people are repelled by Hyde but can't say why – they don't recognise that he is 'pure evil'.

AO2: Stevenson presents this assessment of the evil embodied in Hyde through Jekyll's point of view and words, and Jekyll himself says it is not necessarily truth but only his idea of what is 'most probable'.

AO2: Jekyll uses the words 'good' and 'evil' here but he refers to the 'just' and 'unjust' parts of himself when he is first contemplating the potion. The change to more shocking language reflects what he has discovered about himself.

AO2: The simple good/evil division becomes more complex as Jekyll continues. It comes close to a traditional contrast between a virtuous soul and the 'lower elements' (the body) which follow simple appetites. Jekyll's 'every act and thought centered on self' – while he did not set out to be evil, the evil is the result of his selfishness.

AO2: Hyde is associated with the Devil through the language Stevenson uses, but is also associated with animals. 'Satan's signature upon a face' 'masked thing like a monkey jumped'

AO3: Jekyll assumes evil accounts for the ugliness and deformity of Hyde. This reflects a common belief that the moral character of a person could be read in their appearance, the central idea of the pseudo-science of physiognomy, e.g. 'good shone upon the countenance of the one, evil was written broadly and plainly on the face of the other'.

AO3: In separating the parts of himself, Jekyll creates something bizarre and unnatural. The unnatural is a common concern of Gothic literature, a genre with which the novel is closely aligned, e.g. 'Edward Hyde, alone in the ranks of mankind, was pure evil.'